Collins

KS3
History

Revision Guide

Philippa Birch, Steve McDonald,
Rachelle Pennock and Alf Wilkinson

About this Revision & Practice Book

When it comes to getting the best results, practice really does make perfect!

Experts have proved that repeatedly testing yourself on a topic is far more effective than re-reading information over and over again. And, to be as effective as possible, you should space out the practice test sessions over time. This Complete Revision & Practice book is specially designed to support this approach to revision.

Revise

These pages provide a recap of everything you need to know for each topic.

You should read through all the information before taking the Quick Test at the end. This will test whether you can recall the key facts.

> **Quick Test**
>
> 1. Which archbishop did Henry II quarrel with?
> 2. When was the archbishop killed?
> 3. Why might a criminal go on a Crusade?
> 4. Who was Saladin?
> 5. Who was known as the Lionheart?

Practise

These topic-based questions appear shortly after the revision pages for each topic and will test whether you have understood the topic. If you get any of the questions wrong, make sure you read the correct answer carefully.

Review

These topic-based questions appear later in the book, allowing you to revisit the topic and test how well you have remembered the information. If you get any of the questions wrong, make sure you read the correct answer carefully.

Mix it Up

These pages feature a mix of questions, just like you would get in a test. They will make sure you can recall the relevant information to answer a question without being told which topic it relates to.

Test Yourself on the Go

Visit our website at **collins.co.uk/collinsks3revision** and print off a set of flashcards. These pocket-sized cards feature questions and answers so that you can test yourself on all the key facts anytime and anywhere. You will also find lots more information about the advantages of spaced practice and how to plan for it.

Workbook

This section features even more topic-based and mixed test-style questions, providing two further practice opportunities for each topic to guarantee the best results.

ebook

To access the ebook, visit collins.co.uk/ebooks and follow the step-by-step instructions.

QR Codes

Found throughout the book, the QR codes can be scanned on your smartphone for extra practice and explanations.

A QR code in the Revise section links to a Quick Recall Quiz on that topic. A QR code in the Workbook section links to a video working through the solution to one of the questions on that topic.

Contents

Review Questions

KS2 Key Concepts

Where necessary, write or continue your answers on a separate piece of paper.

1 Place the following events in the correct chronological order.

a) The Roman invasion of Britain by Claudius.

b) Augustine's mission sets up Christianity in Britain.

c) Iron Age hill forts are built in Britain.

d) Alfred the Great rules England.

e) Boudicca's uprising against the Romans. [5]

2 Fill in the blanks in the sentences using the words below.

Lindisfarne	Anglo-Saxon	Roman	St Cuthbert	Before

Julius Caesar was a _____ general. He invaded Britain in 55 BCE, which stands for _____ the Common Era.

Alfred the Great was an _____ king. He created peace between the Vikings and the English.

_____ was a Christian monk. He brought Christianity to northern England. He built a big

monastery on an island off the east coast of northern England called _____ [5]

3 Look back at question 2. Who do you think was **most** important out of Julius Caesar, Alfred the Great and St Cuthbert? Make sure you give a reason for your answer. [2]

4 Look back at question 2. Who do you think was **least** important out of Julius Caesar, Alfred the Great and St Cuthbert? Make sure you give a reason for your answer. [2]

5 Read the sources below then answer the questions.

> *Source A: A modern historian's view*
>
> In today's society, nobody would be allowed to work in such awful conditions. Injuries such as the loss of fingers and hands, beatings from factory owners, and death were common. It is shocking that children were allowed to work in this type of setting.

Source B: Part of a factory owner's account after the passing of the Factory Act in 1833, which improved conditions for workers

Working in factories is very beneficial for children. They are provided with food and water; they cannot work more than 48 hours per week and any child under the age of eleven receives two hours of schooling per day.

a) Using Source A, describe what conditions were like in factories during the Victorian period. [3]

b) Compare Sources A and B. How are they different? Give an example from both sources. [4]

c) Look at the origin of Source B (who wrote it). Why do you think the factory owner would want to show that conditions weren't as bad as people thought? [3]

6   In 1939, just under 1 million children from English cities such as London and Manchester were evacuated to the countryside for safety. Look at the photograph below then answer the questions.

a) How can you tell that these children are evacuees? [2]

b) Give examples of two effects that evacuation might have on:

   i)   mothers who are sending their children away

   ii) children who are being sent away (evacuees)

   iii) the areas the evacuees have been sent away from. [6]

The Norman Conquest 1

You must be able to:

- Explain why the Norman Conquest was important in English history
- Describe how William the Conqueror won the Battle of Hastings
- Explain the changes made by the feudal system.

What was the Norman Conquest?

- In 1066, major change happened in England.
- The Saxons (originally from Germany) were defeated in battle by a ruler from Normandy in France, who became William I, known as the Conqueror.
- This was the last successful invasion of England.
- Under William the Conqueror, the Norman French became the new rulers of England. They took control of the land and the Church. They introduced a new way of organising the country called the feudal system.
- This change brought about the start of the Middle Ages in England, a period of history that would last for 500 years.

> **Key Point**
>
> Normandy was an area of northern France settled by people from Norway and Denmark, known as Normans from the word 'Norsemen'.

How did William Win the Battle of Hastings in 1066?

- Norman rule in England began with their victory at the Battle of Hastings on 14 October 1066.
- When the English king, Edward the Confessor, died on 5 January 1066, Harold became the new Saxon English king. Harold was the most powerful earl in England and the leaders of England wanted a strong king.
- William of Normandy felt he had a claim to the English throne after his cousin Edward had apparently promised him the crown in 1051. He was supported by the Pope, who was head of the Church in Europe.
- William invaded England by crossing the Channel from Normandy.
- At the same time, Harald Hardrada, King of Norway and Denmark, invaded northern England from Denmark. Harthacnut, the Viking king of England from 1040–1042, had promised the throne to Harald's father before he died. After the death of his father, Harald claimed he should be king of England.
- The Saxon English king, Harold, marched his army to the north of England to fight Harald Hardrada first. The Danes were defeated at Stamford Bridge in Yorkshire and Harold's army then marched all the way south to fight William near Hastings.

William the Conqueror

- The Saxons fought well but Harold was killed.
- William of Normandy won the Battle of Hastings after playing a trick and pretending to retreat. He then marched on towards London and, on 25 December 1066, was crowned King William I.
- A description of the battle was embroidered on cloth. It is called the Bayeux Tapestry, after the town in Normandy where it was made.
- The tapestry shows the main events of William's invasion of England and the Battle of Hastings. It was made over a decade after the battle.

Battle scene from the Bayeux Tapestry

What was the Feudal System?

- The biggest change the Normans made in England was to introduce a new way of organising society, known as the feudal system.
- Under the feudal system King William I owned all the land in England.
- The King kept one-quarter of the land for his own use and gave the rest to his main supporters, barons and bishops.
- About 200 barons and bishops controlled three-quarters of England's land. They gave land to about 400 knights, who gave service to their barons in times of war.
- Most of the work in England was done by 1.5 million peasants. They were allowed small plots of land. In return they had to work for the baron when required.
- These peasants were called villeins. They employed poorer peasants called bordars and cottars.
- The feudal system meant that power in England was centred on the King and his barons and bishops. Most Saxons lost their land.

> **Key Point**
>
> Villeins were farm labourers or peasants who had to work several days each year for their baron in return for small plots of land.

Quick Test

1. In what year was the Battle of Hastings?
2. Who was the King of the Saxons at this time?
3. Of which English king did William claim to be a distant relative?
4. What is the name of the famous tapestry that depicts the Battle of Hastings?
5. What is the name given to the system for organising society introduced by the Normans?

The Norman Conquest 2

You must be able to:

- Describe the rebellions against William the Conqueror
- Explain why castles helped the Normans to gain control
- Explain why the Domesday Book was important.

Quick Recall Quiz

How did William Use Castles to Control England?

- When William I became king, he established control of England.
- In England, there were 1.5 million Saxon English and only 10 000 Normans.
- The Saxons did not want to be ruled by the French.
- There were rebellions by Saxons across England, including a rebellion in northern England in 1069.
- The most serious rebellion took place in eastern England, in an area known as the Fens. A Saxon lord, Hereward the Wake, fought the Normans for over a decade after 1066 before he was defeated.
- Further resistance occurred in the south-west. This was led by Lady Gytha, the mother of King Harold. The Domesday Book showed that she was the richest woman in England in 1066. After William became King, she inspired the 1068 rebellion in Exeter. When Exeter was defeated, she fled to Flat Holme, an island in the Bristol Channel, before going to Denmark to live with relatives.
- William kept control by building castles across England.
- Norman castles followed a standard pattern:
  - A small hill was created called a motte and this was surrounded by a wooden fence and a moat.
  - An outer area, called a bailey, was also surrounded by a wooden fence. This contained housing. Later, the wooden fences were replaced by stone.
- Castles were the homes of lords and knights.
- The castles were easy to defend and showed the Saxon English that the Normans were in control.

> ### Key Point
>
> Motte and bailey is the type of castle built across England by the Normans as a way to keep control.

Durham Castle is an example of a Norman castle

The Domesday Book 1086

- In the winter of 1085–86 William I did something extraordinary that had never been done before. He made a survey of all the land in England and recorded it in the Domesday Book.
- William sent officials around the country to ask questions about who owned land and what the land was worth.

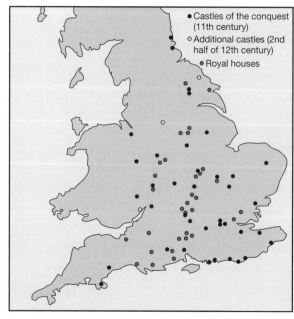

- Castles of the conquest (11th century)
- Additional castles (2nd half of 12th century)
- Royal houses

Locations of Norman castles by the end of the 12th century

- All answers were double checked on a second visit.
- Over 13 000 places were visited.
- Normally six villagers and their leader, known as a reeve, were asked the questions.
- The Domesday Book mentions almost all of England's villages and records the value of their land.
- This gave William information about the wealth of his kingdom. It also showed the wealth of each of his lords and bishops.
- This was important because it showed William how much tax he could claim from each lord and bishop.

A volume of the Domesday Book

- William I died on 9 September 1087, having defeated the Saxon English, built castles across England and established control of the country.

Timeline

1066 Battle of Hastings; William is crowned king.
1066–76 Rebellion of Hereward the Wake.
1069 Rebellion against William I in northern England.
1085–86 Domesday Book compiled.
1087 William I dies.

Quick Test

1. Where did rebellions take place against Norman rule?
2. Who led a Saxon rebellion for over a decade?
3. What was the small hill called on which Normans built their castles?
4. What was the name of the book that contained William's survey of England?
5. In what year did William die?

Christendom and the Crusades 1

You must be able to:

- Describe how religion was organised in the Middle Ages
- Explain why religion was important to people
- Explain why the Church was so powerful.

Why was Religion so Important in the Middle Ages?

- In the Middle Ages, religion was the most important thing in most people's lives.
- The vast majority of people were illiterate (unable to read) and looked to religion as a way to organise their lives.
- The fear of death was felt by everyone in a time when there was only basic medical knowledge and for most people life was nasty, brutish and short.
- Virtually everyone in England at this time was Christian.
- There was also a very small population of Jews.
- Christianity was divided into two parts:
  - In Western Europe, the Christian Church looked to the Pope in Rome as leader.
  - In Eastern Europe, people followed Orthodox Christianity and looked to the Emperor of Byzantium as leader.
- The whole area under Christian rule was called Christendom.

Key Point

Byzantium was a Christian empire in Eastern Europe centred on Constantinople, now known as Istanbul. It covered the area east of Italy and south of Ukraine.

Organisation of the Churches and Monasteries

- In England, the head of the country was the King, supported by barons and knights.
- The Christian Church had its own organisational structure.
- The Head of the Western Church was the Pope, in Rome, Italy.
- The Pope was chosen by senior churchmen called cardinals.
- In England, the most senior churchman was the Archbishop of Canterbury.
- Below him were bishops who organised the Church across England in areas known as dioceses.
- Within each diocese were hundreds of parishes, each led by a parish priest who performed religious services in a church.
- There were also monasteries and convents where religious people worked and prayed. These were led by abbots and abbesses.
- These looked after monks, nuns and friars, who were religious people who chose to live in monasteries and convents to pray and to do good works.

Key Point

Monasteries were religious houses for men and convents were religious houses for women.

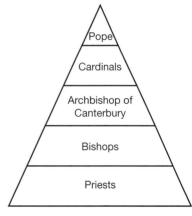

Organisation of the Church

Why was the Christian Church so Powerful?

- The Christian Church owned large amounts of land, making it rich and powerful.
- Monasteries and churches employed thousands of people to help the bishops, priests and monks.
- Life was unpredictable, with a constant fear of disease and death, but many believed that the Church offered a route to everlasting life in heaven.
- Even the King and lords looked to the Church to help them get to heaven.
- One of the Pope's greatest powers was his ability to excommunicate people, even kings.
- Excommunicants were no longer members of the Church, and it was believed that when they died they would go to hell, a place ruled by the Devil.
- Many believed that people in hell would face everlasting punishment and pain.
- Many English kings and lords at this time were illiterate, like the vast majority of the population.
- The Church was home to priests and monks who could read and write. They were employed by the King and lords to help them administer their lands.
- One of the only ways ordinary people could leave their town or village would be by going on a pilgrimage.
- A pilgrimage is a journey to a religious place, usually associated with a holy person whose remains or relics could be seen.
- Pilgrimages were regarded as a help in the quest for heaven.

A stained glass window of a monk

> **Key Point**
>
> Many beliefs held by Christians in the Middle Ages are still upheld by people today.

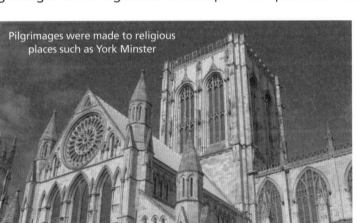

Pilgrimages were made to religious places such as York Minster

---

Quick Test

1. Who was head of the Western Christian Church?
2. Who was the most senior churchman in England?
3. Who lived and worked in monasteries and convents?
4. What did it mean to be excommunicated?
5. Why did people want to go on pilgrimages?

Christendom and the Crusades 2

Quick Recall Quiz

You must be able to:

- Describe why Henry II and Thomas A'Becket quarrelled
- Explain why the Crusades took place
- Explain who won the Crusades.

The Struggle for Power Between the King and the Church

- The King and the Church usually worked well together.
- The Church enjoyed the protection of the King and gave its support to him.
- The King enjoyed the support of the Church and the work of literate bishops and monks.
- In the late 12th century, a conflict developed between King Henry II and the Archbishop of Canterbury, Thomas A'Becket.
- A'Becket had once been Henry's chief minister.
- When he became archbishop, A'Becket wanted the Church to be separate from the King, in particular in courts of law. A'Becket supported separate Church Courts for priests and monks. Henry wanted the clergy to be tried in the same courts as ordinary people to ensure fairness.
- In 1170, some knights murdered A'Becket in Canterbury Cathedral.
- They thought they were acting for the King, but there was outrage. Henry II felt very guilty and volunteered to be punished – he was flogged in public.
- A'Becket was made a saint, or holy man of the Church, and Canterbury became a place of pilgrimage.

Why did the Crusades Take Place?

- The Crusades were a series of wars between Christians and Muslims over control of the Holy Land, modern-day Israel.
- The main goal of the Crusades was to capture Jerusalem, the city where Jesus was crucified.
- The Crusades began in the late 11th century and lasted hundreds of years.
- The Pope hoped the Crusades would make the Church even more powerful.
- People went on Crusades for many reasons:
  - Some kings and lords were seeking money and power.
  - Others believed it would get them into heaven when they died.
  - Criminals and thieves went to escape punishment.

> **Key Point**
>
> As priests and monks made up the vast majority of those who were literate (able to read and write) this gave the Church much power.

In 1170, Thomas A'Becket was killed in Canterbury Cathedral

> **Key Point**
>
> After death, Christians believe good people go to heaven, where they achieve everlasting happiness. The opposite of heaven is hell.

Who Won the Crusades?

- In 1099, the Crusaders captured Jerusalem and created a Christian kingdom in the Holy Land.
- Within 100 years Muslims had recaptured most of the Holy Land.
- Salah u Din, known as Saladin, was a major Muslim warrior king who controlled the Holy Land between 1174 and 1193.
- In 1187, he won a great victory over the Crusaders at the Battle of Hattin.
- One of Saladin's main Christian opponents was the English King Richard I, who was known as Richard the Lionheart. He fought Saladin in the Third Crusade (1189–1192) but failed to capture Jerusalem.
- In 1212, there was even a Children's Crusade when 30 000 children from France and Germany tried to reach Jerusalem. Many of the children were sold into slavery by fellow Christians.
- Although the Crusaders had some success and ruled the Holy Land for part of the Middle Ages, for most of the time the area was controlled by Muslims.
- Despite the ongoing fighting, Christians and Muslims also depended on each other for trade. Acre was an important city during the Crusades and the site of several battles. Saladin took it in 1191, only for it to be retaken and held by the Crusaders for the next 100 years. Acre then became a major trade centre between East and West – silks, spices, olive oil and sugar from the East met woollen goods and saffron from the West.

Saladin

Key Point

Jerusalem is a holy city for Christians, Muslims and Jews.

Crusaders and Muslims at war

Quick Test

1. Which archbishop did Henry II quarrel with?
2. When was the archbishop killed?
3. Why might a criminal go on a Crusade?
4. Who was Saladin?
5. Who was known as the Lionheart?

Timeline

1096–99 The First Crusade.
1147–49 The Second Crusade.
1170 Archbishop Thomas A'Becket murdered in Canterbury.
1187 Battle of Hattin.
1189–92 The Third Crusade.
1202–04 The Fourth Crusade.
1212 The Children's Crusade.

Magna Carta 1

You must be able to:

- Describe the problems facing King John
- Explain why John had problems with the barons and the Church
- Explain what Magna Carta was.

Quick Recall Quiz

What Problems did King John Face?

- King John replaced his brother Richard I, known as the Lionheart, in 1199 after Richard was killed in France.
- John had acted as regent during Richard's Crusade to the Holy Land, along with his mother, Eleanor of Aquitaine, who was one of the most powerful women of the period. Formerly married to King Louis of France, she later married Henry II of England and played an active part in running his empire until 1173, when she supported her sons' attempt to overthrow their father. The revolt failed and she spent the next 16 years in prison, until Richard succeeded to the throne and released her. Although her involvement in England ended on Richard's death, she remained active in the affairs of Aquitaine until she died in 1204 at 82.
- Richard I had left England in a great deal of debt due to wars with France and the Third Crusade.
- Richard I had been a great warrior king while John was regarded as weak. His nickname was 'John soft sword'.
- When he became King of England, John had problems controlling his lands in Wales and Ireland.
- John also faced attacks from Scotland, which was an independent country.
- During most of his reign, England was at war with France.
- By 1204, John had lost most of England's territories in France, such as Normandy.

> **Key Point**
>
> When John became King, England also ruled Wales, most of Ireland and a large part of northern France.

Statue of Richard the Lionheart, outside the Houses of Parliament in London

Problems with the Church

- In 1205, the Pope appointed Stephen Langton as Archbishop of Canterbury, the most senior position in the English Church.
- John disliked Stephen Langton and wanted his own choice of archbishop.
- In 1205, the Pope, Innocent III, stopped all religious ceremonies such as marriages and burials in England. This lasted for six years.
- John, in return, took money from the Church and expelled monks from England.
- In 1209, the Pope excommunicated John, which meant John was no longer a member of the Church.
- This quarrel seriously weakened John's position as king.

King John

Problems with the Barons

- Barons were the most powerful people in England, after the King. They owned most of the land and provided most of King John's army.
- Barons expected their king to be a good warrior and to involve them in running the country.
- John was a poor warrior who tried to rule on his own.
- He also gave top jobs in his government to foreigners rather than barons.
- John's wars with France, Scotland, Wales and Ireland were very costly and the King expected the barons to pay extra taxes to fund them.

Was King John a bad king?

- The majority of historians would argue that King John was a bad king. He was seen as weaker than his predecessor Richard the Lionheart. For most of his reign he was in conflict with the two most powerful groups in England: the barons and the Church.
- Some historians would argue that King John was not as bad as people have made out.
- John was a very good organiser and manager.
- He was very intelligent and good at planning military tactics.

Magna Carta Memorial, Runnymede

What was Magna Carta?

- Magna Carta was a charter signed in 1215 at Runnymede, an island in the River Thames, west of London.
- Magna Carta is Latin for 'Great Charter'. Latin was the language used in government in England at the time.
- The charter was an agreement between King John and the most senior landowners in England, the barons.
- The agreement limited the powers of the English King and protected the rights of the barons.
- It also gave Englishmen certain important civil rights such as trial by a jury of fellow Englishmen.
- It is regarded as one of the most important documents in English history and helped lead to the creation of the national parliament we have today.

> ### Quick Test
>
> 1. What was John's nickname?
> 2. What was the name of the Archbishop of Canterbury appointed by the Pope in 1205?
> 3. What actions did the Pope take against King John?
> 4. How did King John try to punish the Church?
> 5. What does Magna Carta mean in English?

Quick Recall Quiz

Magna Carta 2

You must be able to:

- Explain why King John agreed to Magna Carta
- Describe the changes made by Magna Carta
- Explain the importance of Magna Carta in English history.

Why King John Signed Magna Carta

- By 1214, John had fought wars with France, Wales, Ireland and Scotland.
- In 1214, he lost Poitou, an area of France that had been controlled by England.
- For six years, churches were closed on the orders of the Pope. People were worried that they would go to hell as a result.
- In 1214, King John went to war against the barons.
- The extra taxes that John demanded had forced the barons to rebel and form their own army.
- In May 1215, the barons captured London.
- In June, the barons forced King John to sign an agreement at Runnymede, near Windsor, west of London.
- This was Magna Carta, or Great Charter.
- King John hoped that signing Magna Carta would stop the barons' rebellion.

> **Key Point**
>
> By 1215, John had fallen out with the barons and the Church and had been defeated in war by France.

What Changes did Magna Carta Make?

- Magna Carta made changes to King John's relations with the Church, the barons and ordinary people.
- The first part of Magna Carta stated that the King would not interfere with the Church.
- The next part stated that when a baron inherited land he should not pay more than £100 to the King.
- Another important part said that the King could not raise any new taxes without the agreement of the barons and bishops.
- Freemen could not be put in prison without a trial by a jury of freemen.
- The King's judges had to be fair to everyone.
- Everyone was free to enter or leave England. They did not need the King's permission.

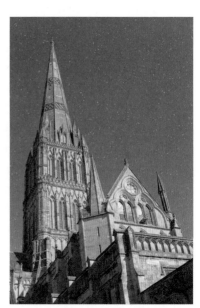

A copy of Magna Carta is kept in Salisbury Cathedral

The Importance of Magna Carta

- Magna Carta was the first time an English King had agreed to protect the rights of Englishmen in writing.
- It was important because the King no longer ruled without the support of the barons and the Church.
- It gave freemen (people who were not villeins) in England certain rights.
- Magna Carta protected the rights of the rich and powerful barons and the Church.
- Most Englishmen were not freemen but villeins, so were unaffected by Magna Carta.

The Creation of Parliament

- If a king wanted to raise taxes, he had to consult his Great Council, made up of barons and bishops.
- Under John's son, King Henry III, England's first Parliament was called in 1265 by Simon de Montfort.
- This Parliament contained barons, bishops, two knights from each county and town representatives.
- Barons and bishops formed the House of Lords.
- Knights and townspeople formed the House of Commons. The members of the House of Commons were elected.
- These changes laid the foundations of the Houses of Parliament we have today.

The Houses of Parliament today

Timeline

1199 John becomes King.
1204 King John loses Normandy to France.
1205 John has a major argument with the Pope.
1209 The Pope excommunicates John.
1214 War breaks out between John and the barons.
1215 John signs Magna Carta.
1265 England's first Parliament meets.

Quick Test

1. In what year did the barons capture London?
2. Where was Magna Carta signed?
3. After Magna Carta was introduced, what was the maximum amount a baron had to pay the King when he inherited land?
4. Who formed the House of Lords?
5. Who formed the House of Commons?

The Black Death 1

You must be able to:

- Explain the real cause of the Black Death
- Describe how people died of the Black Death
- Explain what people at the time thought caused the Black Death.

Quick Recall Quiz

What was the Black Death?

- The Black Death was a severe outbreak of disease that affected England from 1348 to 1350.
- It was bubonic plague and was spread by fleas carried by black rats.
- The disease is thought to have originated in China and was brought to England by black rats on boats from Europe. At first it spread along trade routes such as the Silk Road which brought goods to Europe from China and India.
- It spread from the ports all over the country within a year and had a devastating effect on England.
- The Black Death killed about one-third of the population – 1.5 million people died out of a population of 4 million.
- About 25 million people died in Europe.
- In China the population dropped from 125 million to just 65 million in 50 years because of the Black Death.
- In England, 7 500 people a day died of the Black Death.
- Everyone was affected – old and young, rich and poor.
- Even King Edward III's daughter, Joan, died of the disease.

> ### Key Point
>
> The bubonic plague caused the Black Death. People who caught the disease suffered severe flu symptoms, coughing, and swollen lumps on the arms and legs.

The Black Death was spread by fleas on black rats

Beliefs about the Black Death

- Although the Black Death was brought to England by rats on ships, it was the fleas that lived on the rats that caused the disease.
- In the Middle Ages, people lived in primitive conditions and had very poor hygiene.
- Modern-day toilets and waste disposal did not exist. Sewage flowed in the streets, which led to the rapid spread of disease.
- Although doctors now know how the disease spread, in 1348 the vast majority of people were illiterate and very little was known about the causes of disease.
- Many people thought the disease was a punishment from God and therefore felt that if they prayed a lot it would save them. Others whipped themselves as a form of punishment to please God.

- A popular idea was that the end of the world was coming. Venus, Mars and Jupiter were all seen together in the sky in 1348, making people think a disaster was going to happen.
- A popular belief was that the disease was spread by 'bad air'.
- The authorities tried to improve the situation by clearing the streets of rubbish and lighting fires to disperse the bad air that they thought spread the disease. They also confined victims to their own homes.
- Individuals:
  - sat next to large fires in the hope they would destroy the bad air
  - placed sweet-smelling dried flowers and herbs over their nose and mouth to prevent the bad air from entering their body
  - used dried toads and leeches to remove the poison from diseased bodies
  - rubbed raw onion or placed figs and butter on the swollen lumps to soften and reduce them
  - believed that rubbing themselves all over with vinegar, or drinking it, would stop them catching the Black Death.
- Doctors would take blood from the sick patient – bad blood was thought to cause the plague and many other diseases.

Figs were placed on swollen lumps

Butter was used to soften the swollen lumps

Treating a sufferer of the Black Death

Quick Test

1. When was the first outbreak of the Black Death?
2. How did the Black Death get to England?
3. How did people get the disease?
4. How many people died of the Black Death in Europe?
5. Which animals did people use to treat the Black Death?

The Black Death 2

You must be able to:

- Describe the symptoms of the Black Death
- Explain the immediate impact of the Black Death
- Explain how the Black Death affected England in the following 100 years.

Symptoms of the Black Death

- People learnt to identify the symptoms of the Black Death through observation.
- To begin with, victims suffered from flu symptoms of sweating and coughing.
- Then large lumps appeared on their bodies, usually on the arms and legs.
- These lumps, or buboes, were red at first, because they were full of blood, but then turned black, giving the disease its name. The lumps went black as the blood in the body dried out.
- Victims suffered high temperatures.
- Blotches appeared all over the body.
- Most people who caught the Black Death died within five days.

Social Effects of the Black Death

- Whole villages and towns were wiped out by the Black Death.
- The population of England dropped by about one-third in two years because of the disease.
- People began leaving towns and going to live in the countryside in an attempt to avoid it.
- Foreigners and non-Christians, such as Jews, were attacked because some people blamed them for causing the disease.
- Jews were forced to live in separate parts of towns and some people were banned altogether.

Economic Effects of the Black Death

- With fewer peasants, much agricultural land was unused.
- Peasants left their fields and unattended livestock were left to die.
- Food supplies started to run low and prices rose.
- As there were fewer peasants to work the land and fewer craftsmen in towns, these people began to demand higher wages.
- Villeins began to refuse to work on the lord's land for free. They disliked this obligation and resented having to pay taxes.
- Lords offered villeins more food and money to work their land, so those who survived benefited from the changes brought by the Black Death.

> **Key Point**
>
> The loss of one-third of the population saw hundreds of villages abandoned. New towns developed as people moved to different areas.

Livestock died as a result of fewer peasants to take care of them

The Next 100 Years

- During the 50 years following the Black Death, many villages were abandoned as their populations dropped so severely that village life could not survive.
- Hundreds of villages disappeared. Several of these lost villages were rediscovered in the 20th century through aerial photography.
- Many people began to lose faith in the Christian Church.
- They had been told that the Black Death was a punishment from God but churchmen and those who prayed also died.
- There were fewer people to provide religious help as 40 per cent of priests and monks had died of the Black Death.
- In 1349 a law was passed, the Ordinance of Labourers, that tried to keep wages at pre-Black Death levels, but it was ignored.
- The loss of population led to the need for more machines to help produce goods such as cloth.
- When the Poll Tax was introduced in 1381, 30 years after the Black Death, a major rebellion took place called the Peasants' Revolt.

Key Point

The Black Death returned roughly every 10 years and the population of England declined over the following 100 years.

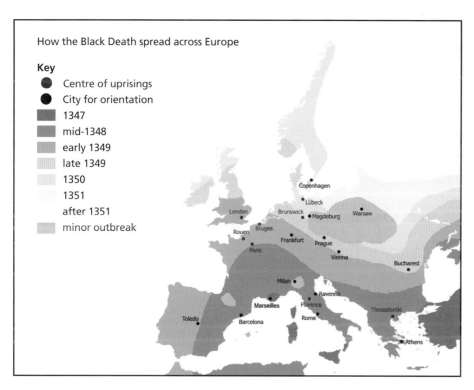

How the Black Death spread across Europe

Key
- ● Centre of uprisings
- ● City for orientation
- ■ 1347
- ■ mid-1348
- ■ early 1349
- ■ late 1349
- ■ 1350
- ■ 1351
- ■ after 1351
- ▒ minor outbreak

Copenhagen
Lübeck
London Brunswick Magdeburg Warsaw
Rouen Bruges
Frankfurt Prague
Paris
Vienna
Bucharest
Milan
Ravenna
Marseilles Florence
Toledo Barcelona Rome Thessaloniki
Athens

Quick Test

1. What were the symptoms of the Black Death?
2. How long did people who caught the Black Death normally survive?
3. Which group of people were blamed and forced to live in separate parts of town?
4. How did the Black Death affect food prices?
5. How were the surviving villeins affected after the Black Death?

Timeline

June 1348 Black Death arrives in England at Melcombe Regis (Weymouth) in Dorset.
Aug 1348 Black Death hits Bristol.
Sept 1348 Black Death reaches London.
Jan 1349 Parliament stops meeting because of the plague.
Jan–Feb 1349 Black Death spreads into East Anglia and the Midlands.
April 1349 Black Death reported in Wales.
July 1349 Black Death hits Ireland.

Practice Questions

The Norman Conquest

1 Which country did the Saxons come from before they came to England?

.... [1]

2 Which part of France was William the Conqueror originally from?

.... [1]

3 Who led the Danes in the fight against the Saxons at Stamford Bridge?

.... [1]

4 What was a 'bailey'?

.... [1]

5 Why could William lay claim to the English throne?

In your answer you should:
- Give your opinion of William's three most important claims.
- Provide any other reason(s) William had a claim.
- Support your answer with facts and figures.

Write your answer on a separate sheet of paper. [10]

6 Why do you think William won the Battle of Hastings?

In your answer you should:
- Say why the Normans were in a better position than the Saxons.
- State some of the problems the Saxons faced.
- Use your own knowledge to support your answer.

Write your answer on a separate sheet of paper. [10]

Christendom and the Crusades

1 Who led the Orthodox Christians in the East of Europe?

_____ [1]

2 What town became a place of pilgrimage following Thomas A'Becket's death?

_____ [1]

3 What city in the Middle East were the Crusaders trying to capture?

_____ [1]

4 What was a pilgrimage?

_____ [1]

5 Imagine you are a villein in the Middle Ages. Explain why religion is important to you.

In your answer you should:
* Describe your life and what you do.
* Give at least two reasons why religion is important in your life.

Write your answer on a separate sheet of paper. [10]

6 In the Middle Ages, in what ways were the lives of priests and monks different?

In your answer you should:
* Give descriptions, in turn, of what priests and monks did in the Middle Ages.
* Use your own knowledge and evidence to explain how the lives of priests and monks were different.

Write your answer on a separate sheet of paper. [10]

Practice Questions

Magna Carta

1 When was Magna Carta signed?

.... [1]

2 What did Magna Carta limit?

.... [1]

3 What important civil right did Magna Carta give Englishmen?

.... [1]

4 What did the Pope do to King John in 1209?

.... [1]

5 Why have people seen King John as a weak king? Do you agree that he was weak?

In your answer you should:
- Give your opinion, backed up with facts and figures.
- Explain why people, at the time and since, have thought John was weak.

Write your answer on a separate sheet of paper. [10]

6 Why do you think the barons had a quarrel with King John?

In your answer you should:
- Give at least three reasons, supported with facts and figures.
- Explain why these reasons caused the quarrel.
- Write at least two paragraphs: the first dealing with reasons caused by King John, and the second dealing with reasons caused by others.

Write your answer on a separate sheet of paper. [10]

The Black Death

1 How many people died each day of the Black Death in England?

.... [1]

2 What gave the disease its name?

.... [1]

3 How often did the Black Death reoccur in the 100 years after 1350?

.... [1]

4 How did villeins benefit from the Black Death?

.... [1]

5 Why were the symptoms of the Black Death so unpleasant?

In your answer you should:
* Give your opinion of why the symptoms were so unpleasant.
* Describe two of the worst symptoms.

Write your answer on a separate sheet of paper. [10]

6 How did people try to stop the spread of the Black Death in England?

In your answer you should:
* Explain how each method was intended to stop the spread of the disease.
* Write two paragraphs: the first dealing with religious ideas about the spread of the disease, and the second dealing with non-religious ideas.

Write your answer on a separate sheet of paper. [10]

The Peasants' Revolt 1

You must be able to:

- Describe the problems facing Richard II
- Explain how the war with France affected England
- Give reasons why the revolt took place.

England under Richard II

- Richard II became King in 1377 after the death of his grandfather, Edward III.
- He was only 10 years old in 1377 so England was ruled by his advisers.
- Unfortunately, this group of advisers did not include England's most important lord, John of Gaunt.
- Following the Black Death, when one-third of the population died, England was short of wealth.
- England ruled a large part of France, Wales and Ireland.
- Richard had inherited a very costly war against the French.
- The Hundred Years War against France was becoming more expensive to fight each year.

> **Key Point**
>
> When Richard II became King he was too young to rule on his own. A council of senior advisers was created that made all major decisions.

What was the Peasants' Revolt of 1381?

- The Peasants' Revolt in 1381 was the most serious rebellion in the Middle Ages.
- There were many reasons for the revolt including the introduction of Poll Tax and peasants wanting fairer rights.
- It started in Fobbing in Essex, and was centred on counties close to London, most notably Essex and Kent.

Areas affected by the Peasants' Revolt

- The rebels entered London and came very close to overthrowing the government.
- The defeat of the Peasants' Revolt saved the reign of young King Richard II.
- To end the revolt, Richard made many promises to the rebels, which he subsequently failed to keep.
- Although the King and lords triumphed, the shortage of labour after the Black Death meant that wages actually rose.

Causes of the Peasants' Revolt

- There were many causes of the Peasants' Revolt in 1381.
- The immediate cause of the revolt was the introduction of Poll Tax in 1380.
- Poll Tax was a tax paid by all adult men.
  - The tax was needed to pay for the ongoing war against France (the Hundred Years War).
  - Everyone, rich and poor, was charged the same amount of tax: five pence per person in England.
  - Peasants feared new taxes after the introduction of Poll Tax. There had already been tax rises in 1377, 1379 and 1380.
- After the Black Death there was a shortage of peasants and this led to their demands for wages.
  - At this time, peasants still worked for lords for no pay.
  - Many peasants had to work for free on Church land, sometimes for up to two days a week.
  - This meant that they could not work their own land, which made it difficult to feed their families.
  - Peasants wanted to be free of this burden, which made the Church rich at their expense.
- John Ball, a priest from Kent, said that God had not created rich and poor. Everyone should be seen as equal.
- Richard II was only 14 years old so the peasants believed he had been given poor advice by the Chancellor, Simon of Sudbury, and the Royal Treasurer, Sir Robert Hales.
- The rebellion was more against Richard II's advisers than the young king.

Richard II

The Peasants' Revolt 2

You must be able to:

- Describe the main events of the Peasants' Revolt
- Explain how Richard II brought the revolt to an end
- Explain the effects of the revolt on England.

Main Events of the Revolt

- In May 1381, a tax collector arrived in the Essex village of Fobbing to find out why people had not paid the Poll Tax. He was thrown out by the villagers.
- In the same month, in Kent, some peasants seized a castle. They recognised Wat Tyler as their leader, the man who was to become head of the revolt.
- Soldiers were then sent to Fobbing in June.
- In response, the Fobbing peasants organised themselves into armed groups, which were supported by other Essex villages.
- This started an armed rebellion across Essex, which also spread to Kent.
- On 11 June, Kentish peasants marched on Blackheath, only five miles from London.
    - At the same time, Essex peasants marched on Mile End, just a few miles east of London.
    - In total, there were between 50 000 and 60 000 peasants involved in the revolt.
    - There were also peasant riots in Sussex, Surrey and as far away as Dorset.
- On 12 June, Richard II tried to speak to the peasants, but he failed to deter them.
- On 13 June, the rebels entered London and attacked the homes of the King's advisers.
- On 14 June, Richard II met the Essex rebels at Mile End.
    - Richard II promised to free any rebels from prison, pardon them and punish his advisers.
    - Some rebels murdered the Bishop of London and the Royal Treasurer.
    - They also murdered John Legge, the organiser of the Poll Tax.
- On 15 June, Wat Tyler met Richard II.
    - Tyler demanded that all men should be free and that the Church's wealth should be given to the poor.
    - Tyler was arrested by the Mayor of London, William Walworth, after an argument. Tyler tried to stab the Mayor and was injured in the scuffle.
    - His followers managed to get him to hospital but he was later dragged away and beheaded by order of the Mayor.

Key Point

Peasants were agricultural labourers, most of whom were villeins. As England was mainly an agricultural country they produced most of the country's wealth.

Wat Tyler killing a tax collector

William Walworth killing Wat Tyler

- Richard II agreed to all the rebels' demands. They returned to their homes thinking they had won.
- Apart from putting an end to the Poll Tax, Richard II went on to break all the promises he had made.

Reasons for the Revolt's Failure

- There were several reasons for the failure of the Peasants' Revolt:
  - The rebels lacked discipline and organisation.
  - Most of the rebels accepted Richard II's promises and therefore returned home.
  - Richard had John Ball and many rebel leaders hanged.
  - In Essex and Kent, 8000 royal troops restored order, killing 1500 rebels.
  - The King claimed all his promises were made under threat, so did not count.
  - The rebellion was based mainly in Essex and Kent, not across the whole country.

How Much did England Change After the Peasants' Revolt?

- Although the Peasants' Revolt failed, it did have an impact on the future of life in England.
- The Poll Tax was withdrawn. When it was reintroduced in the late 1980s it caused riots in London in 1990.
- The shortage of labour caused by the Black Death eventually forced lords to pay peasants wages.
- Peasants' living standards rose over the following hundred years.
- The feudal system, which had been introduced by the Normans, began to collapse.
- Richard II, although only 14 years of age, showed great calm during the revolt and won admiration.
- His use of Parliament to raise money saved his rule for a while.
- In 1399, however, he was murdered and replaced by Henry IV.
- By 1500, there were no longer any villeins. All Englishmen were freemen and benefited from the rights in Magna Carta.

Quick Test

1. Who was the leader of the Peasants' Revolt?
2. Where did Richard meet the rebels?
3. What did Richard promise the rebels, which ended the revolt?
4. What was the only promise Richard kept?
5. What happened when the Poll Tax reappeared in the 1980s?

> **Key Point**
>
> The feudal system was a way of organising society introduced in England after 1066. The King granted land to lords and the Church in return for service. In turn, the local lord or the Church gave peasants land for which they had to work several days a week for free as villeins.

The reintroduction of a poll tax caused riots in London in 1990

> **Timeline**
>
> **1377** Richard II becomes King at the age of 10.
> **1380** Poll Tax is introduced.
> **May–June 1381** Peasants' Revolt breaks out in Essex and Kent.
> **1381** Poll Tax is withdrawn.
> **1500** The feudal system ends; all Englishmen are freemen.

Reformation and Counter-Reformation 1

Quick Recall Quiz

You must be able to:

- Explain why the Reformation took place under Henry VIII
- Describe the main changes made under Henry VIII
- Explain how far England had become a Protestant country by 1547.

What were the Reformation and Counter-Reformation?

- In the first half of the 16th century, Europe saw a major split in the Christian Church.
- People began to question the authority of the Pope and the Catholic Church.
- At this time, the Bible, Christianity's holy book, was only available in Latin, but many people wanted to read it in their own language.
- Others wanted to run their own church services.
- These changes first began in Germany, and came to be called the Reformation.
- Those who opposed the Pope and the Catholic Church were known as Protestants.
- The Catholic Church responded by reforming itself and trying to win back lands that had become Protestant. This was called the Counter-Reformation.

> **Key Point**
>
> Catholic refers to the parts of the Western Christian Church that stayed loyal to the Pope. Protestant refers to those areas of Europe that rejected the Pope's authority and wanted new ways of organising the Christian religion.

Henry VIII's Break with Rome

- One of Henry's biggest aims was to have a son who would follow him as king.
- Unfortunately, although his wife, Catherine of Aragon, had six children, including three sons, only one daughter, Mary, survived (later to become Mary I).
- Henry decided to divorce Catherine, who was too old to have any more children, but he needed the support of the Pope to do so.
- The Pope, Clement VII, refused as he was a prisoner of Catherine's nephew, the Holy Roman Emperor Charles V.
- Henry VIII divorced Catherine anyway and married Anne Boleyn in the hope of having a son. She had a daughter, Elizabeth (later to become Elizabeth I).
- He persuaded Parliament to pass the Act of Supremacy in 1534. This made Henry VIII head of the Church in England, which was separate from the Catholic Church headed by the Pope.

John Blanke, a trumpeter, probably came to England with Catherine of Aragon. He played at special occasions for Henry VII and Henry VIII. He is one of around 200 black people known to have lived in Tudor England.

Dissolving the Monasteries

- Henry VIII feared that monastic communities still supported the Pope, even though he had made himself Head of the Church.
- He also wanted the lands and wealth of the monasteries to build up his armed forces.
- Henry ordered a survey to find out how much wealth the monasteries possessed and to show that monks and nuns were not living religious lives.
- In 1536, Henry VIII decided to dissolve (close) the monasteries.
- By 1540, over 800 monasteries had been closed and their wealth taken by Henry and his supporters.
- Opposition to Henry's actions led to a rebellion in 1536 in northern England called the Pilgrimage of Grace.
- Henry defeated the rebellion and executed its leaders, including Robert Aske.

> **Key Point**
>
> Before the Reformation, the Pope chose the Archbishop of Canterbury, and the bishops and abbots of monasteries. Large sums of money were also sent from England to Rome to fund the Pope and Church government. All this stopped in the Reformation.

The ruins of Kirkstall Abbey, Leeds, which was dissolved by Henry VIII

The Church of England under Henry VIII

- Henry changed the way the Church worked in England.
- He appointed the Archbishop of Canterbury and all the bishops, instead of the Pope.
- All churches were ordered to have a Bible in English for people to read.
- Church services were in English rather than Latin.
- England no longer looked to the Pope for guidance and stopped sending him money.

Henry VIII

> **Quick Test**
>
> 1. Before the Reformation, what was the only language in which the Bible was available?
> 2. In what country did the Reformation begin?
> 3. Why did Henry VIII divorce Catherine of Aragon?
> 4. Who did he marry next?
> 5. In what year did Henry begin dissolving the monasteries?

Reformation and Counter-Reformation 2

Quick Recall Quiz

You must be able to:

- Explain the religious changes under Edward VI
- Describe the Counter-Reformation under Mary I.

The Six Articles

- The Church in England was now separate from most of the Christian Church in Europe.
- In 1539, Henry VIII published the Six Articles.
- These set out the religious beliefs of the Church in England and were very similar to those of the Catholic Church.
- Anyone not following the Six Articles faced death. Between 1539 and his death in 1547, Henry executed thousands of Protestants for not following his Six Articles of religious faith.

Edward VI makes England a Protestant Country

- Henry VIII eventually had a son, Edward (later to become Edward VI), with his third wife Jane Seymour.
- When Henry VIII died, Edward VI became king, but he was only nine years old.
- His advisers, most importantly Edward Seymour, Duke of Somerset, decided to make England a more Protestant country.
- In 1549 Edward allowed priests in the Church in England to marry. (Catholic priests are still forbidden from doing so.)
- Priests were no longer expected to wear elaborate robes but simple clothing.
- Edward also introduced a new Book of Common Prayer, written by the Archbishop of Canterbury, Thomas Cranmer.
- The new Book of Common Prayer was written in English and contained new religious services.
- The main Catholic service, the Mass, was abolished. It was replaced by a simple Holy Communion where bread and wine were shared.
- Religious statues and paintings were removed from churches and church walls were whitewashed.
- The Catholic altar was replaced with a simple table as the centre of religious services.
- Edward also closed all remaining monasteries.

> **Key Point**
>
> Catholics believe that in the main part of their religious service, the Mass, the bread and wine offered by a priest actually become the body and blood of Jesus. Protestants believe that their equivalent service is simple and symbolic and reject the Catholic view.

Thomas Cranmer wrote the new Book of Common Prayer in English

The Counter-Reformation under Mary I

- When Edward VI died at the age of 15, he was succeeded by his elder sister Mary I, who had been brought up as a Catholic.
- Mary was determined to bring back the Catholic religion.
- She married Philip of Spain, one of Europe's most important Catholic monarchs.
- She recognised the Pope as Head of the Church in England.
- Protestant bishops and priests were removed and replaced by Catholic ones.
- The Mass returned as the main religious service.
- Many opponents of these Catholic changes were put to death.
- Over 200 Protestants were burnt at the stake, giving Mary I the nickname 'Bloody Mary'.
- Mary I's reign was as short as her brother's. She died in 1558 without a child.
- Mary I was succeeded by her younger sister, Elizabeth I, who had been brought up as a Protestant.
- In 1559, Elizabeth I returned England to being a Protestant country.
- The Counter-Reformation had been shortlived. Since 1558, England has officially been a Protestant country with the monarch as Head of the Church of England.

Key Point

The Counter-Reformation took place across Europe. Catholic countries like Spain executed Protestants and sought to destroy Protestantism wherever it existed.

Mary I

Elizabeth I

Timeline

1509 Henry VIII becomes King.
1533 Henry divorces Catherine of Aragon.
1534 Henry VIII makes himself Supreme Head of the Church in England.
1536 Henry begins closing monasteries.
1547 Edward VI makes England a Protestant country.
1553 Mary I becomes Queen and the Counter-Reformation begins.
1558 Mary I dies and is replaced by the Protestant Elizabeth I.

Quick Test

1. In what year were the Six Articles published?
2. Who was Edward VI's chief adviser?
3. In which language was the Book of Common Prayer written?
4. How did the Protestant religious service differ from the Catholic Mass?
5. Why was Mary I nicknamed 'Bloody Mary'?

The English Civil Wars 1

You must be able to:

- Explain the causes of the English Civil Wars
- Understand who fought on each side
- Understand the significance of the Battle of Edgehill and the Battle of Marston Moor.

What Caused the English Civil Wars?

- Charles I became King in 1625.
- There were many causes of the English Civil Wars which occurred between 1642 and 1648.

Religion

- Charles I was married to a French Roman Catholic, Henrietta Maria.
- William Laud, one of Charles's advisers, introduced unpopular ideas such as burning incense and candles during church services. These were seen as Catholic practices at a time when England was Protestant.
- In 1637, Charles tried to enforce a new prayer book in Scotland.
- Most Members of Parliament were Puritan (strict Protestants), and disapproved of Charles's Catholic connections.

Power

- Charles was often seen as arrogant. He strongly believed in the 'Divine Right of Kings', which meant God had chosen him to be King and no one could question that choice.
- Charles ruled without Parliament between 1629 and 1640. This is known as the 'eleven years of tyranny'.
- Charles used the private Court of the Star Chamber to ruthlessly punish his opponents, and fine people when he was short of money.
- In 1642, Charles attempted to arrest five Members of Parliament, including Oliver Cromwell, on a charge of treason when they refused to give in to his demands.

Money

- Charles was known for his extravagant, expensive lifestyle, which often left him needing more money.
- In 1635, he extended Ship Tax, previously only paid in coastal areas, to the whole country.
- He fought two expensive and unsuccessful wars, with Spain in 1625 and France in 1627.
- After the Scots rebelled in 1640, he was forced to ask Parliament for more money to be able to fight another war.

> ### Key Point
>
> Many of the causes of the civil wars were linked to more than one problem. For example, the problems with Scotland were linked to both religion and money.

Charles I

A Country Divided

- The English Civil Wars were fought by the Royalists (Cavaliers) and Parliamentarians (Roundheads).

Cavaliers	Roundheads
• Supported by most of the gentry	• Mainly merchants and traders
• Often from northern and western regions, with some Irish, Scottish and Welsh soldiers	• Generally from London and the south-east
• Had the better horsemen, or cavalry, hence their name, Cavaliers	• In control of London and the navy, increasing their power
• Generally conservative Protestant or Catholic	• Mainly Puritan, a strict Protestant movement
• Mainly led by Charles's nephew, Prince Rupert	• Latterly led by Oliver Cromwell, who proved himself a key solider

- While the majority of the fighting was done by male soldiers, women also played a part. For example, Lady Mary Bankes twice defended Corfe Castle from a Parliamentary army while Lady Brilliana Harley successfully defended her home, Brampton Bryan, against the Royalists. Dorothy Hazard led the local women in the sandbagging of gaps in the walls during the siege of Bristol by Royalists in 1643.

Battle of Edgehill, 23 October 1642

- War broke out in August 1642, but Edgehill was the first major battle. The two sides stumbled upon each other as Charles marched his army from Shrewsbury to London.
- There was a stalemate situation many times in the battle, with neither side advancing.
- Both sides lost approximately 1500 men, and both declared a victory although there was no clear winner.
- The Cavaliers had intended to continue the battle the following day, but decided against it as their troops were exhausted.

Battle of Marston Moor, 2 July 1644

- This important battle ended any significant Royalist support in the north.
- Prince Rupert had marched into York, a powerful city, quite easily.
- The Royalists' power over York gave them an advantage.
- The battle started to go wrong as the Royalist men arrived bit by bit.
- Their 18000 men were soon outnumbered by 28000 Roundheads, causing them to lose.

> **Key Point**
>
> Having his nephew lead his army, rather than doing it himself, did nothing to improve Charles I's popularity.

Monument at the site of the Battle of Marston Moor

Quick Test

1. Why was Charles I's wife unpopular?
2. What did Charles introduce that angered the Scots?
3. Who led King Charles's army?
4. What was the first major battle of the war?
5. At which battle did Charles lose control of the north of England?

The English Civil Wars 2

Quick Recall Quiz

You must be able to:

- Understand the significance of the Battle of Naseby
- Know what is meant by the Second English Civil War
- Understand the uncertainty around Charles's trial and execution.

Battle of Naseby, 14 June 1645

- Charles's confidence had been boosted by a relatively easy attack on Leicester in May.
- He then decided to try to take Oxford, a key Parliamentarian stronghold.
- He started well but his commanders had become divided.
- Cromwell had developed a 'New Model Army', which was made up of full-time, paid soldiers who could be ordered to serve anywhere in the country.
- Many of Charles's supporters were late as they were travelling from Wales and Somerset. Some never arrived.
- Charles was soon outnumbered by between 8000 and 13000 men.
- Many see the Parliamentarians' victory at Naseby as a turning point in the war.
- Following this battle, in September, Prince Rupert surrendered Bristol to Parliament.
- Charles withdrew his position in the army, and Rupert fled to Holland.

> **Key Point**
>
> The establishment of the New Model Army prior to the Battle of Naseby was a key step in bringing Oliver Cromwell to prominence.

The Second English Civil War

- Following Naseby, there was a series of smaller defeats for the Royalists, but the war was all but over.
- In 1646, Charles gave himself up to the Scots, who eventually surrendered him to Parliament in January 1647.
- Charles fled from Hampton Court Palace, where he was being held, in November 1647.
- Ironically, Charles sided with the Scots, and raised another army, which invaded England. This is sometimes known as the Second English Civil War.
- There were a number of Royalist uprisings, but most were easily put down by the New Model Army.
- The Royalists lacked leadership, money and support. Charles was eventually recaptured in August 1648.

Hampton Court Palace

The Trial of King Charles I

- There had been much discussion about what to do with the captured King.
- Many MPs did not want the King to stand trial.
- Cromwell only allowed MPs into Parliament if he believed they wanted the King to stand trial. This was known as the 'Rump Parliament'.
- However, only 29 of these 46 politicians voted for the King to stand trial.
- The trial started on 1 January 1649.
- Charles was the first monarch ever to be put on trial.
- He was accused of being a 'tyrant, traitor and murderer'.
- Of the 135 judges expected at the trial, only 68 attended.
- The chief judge was John Bradshaw, a lawyer, after no one else was willing to take the job.
- Charles refused to defend himself until after the judgement of the court was read.
- He was found guilty of all charges and sentenced to be executed on 30 January 1649.
- Cromwell's signature can be clearly seen on Charles's death warrant. He is widely rumoured to have been a key supporter in the decision to kill the King.

The Execution of Charles I

- Charles was executed on scaffolding erected outside the Banqueting Hall in London.
- His execution was delayed as the executioner scheduled to carry out the beheading refused to do it.
- It was a struggle to find anyone willing to kill the King.
- Eventually two executioners were paid highly to do the job, on the reassurance they could wear masks throughout so no one would know who they were.
- Charles allegedly wore two shirts as it was a cold day. He did not want to shiver and lead the crowd to believe he was afraid.
- Spectators dipped their handkerchiefs into his blood following the execution owing to the belief that the King's blood had healing powers.

Charles I on trial

 Key Point

An English monarch had never been executed before Charles I, so there was much uncertainty around his trial and execution.

 Timeline

August 1642 War breaks out.
October 1642 Battle of Edgehill.
July 1644 Battle of Marston Moor.
June 1645 Battle of Naseby.
January 1647 Charles is given to Parliament.
November 1647 Charles escapes.
August 1648 Charles is recaptured.
January 1649 Charles is executed.

Quick Test

1. What did Cromwell develop prior to the Battle of Naseby?
2. Which city did Prince Rupert surrender to Parliament?
3. Who did Charles side with after fleeing from Hampton Court Palace?
4. How did Cromwell select MPs for the Rump Parliament?
5. When was Charles's execution?

The Interregnum 1

You must be able to:

- Describe the events leading to Cromwell becoming Lord Protector
- Explain what the republic was
- Explain who the Puritans were.

What is the Interregnum?

- The Interregnum is the period of British history between 1649 and 1660 in which Oliver Cromwell ruled the country as Lord Protector.
- The period began with the execution of Charles I on 30 January 1649 and ended with the restoration of the monarchy by Charles II on 29 May 1660.

England Becomes a Republic

- Following the death of Charles I in January 1649, Parliament passed laws that abolished the monarchy, the House of Lords and the Church of England.
- Parliament declared that England should be a republic. This meant the country would be ruled without a king or queen.
- The most powerful person in the country was Oliver Cromwell.
- Cromwell and most of the army officers were Puritans.
- Parliament did not want to pass the laws that the army wanted, and this caused arguments and tension.
- On 20 April 1653, Cromwell and the army went to Parliament and expelled the MPs.

> ### Key Point
>
> The Puritans believed that God was on their side and that this was the reason for their victory in the Civil Wars. They believed that England should be a more religiously strict country.

The Barebones Parliament

- Oliver Cromwell selected 140 Puritans to become MPs in a new Parliament. This was named the Barebones Parliament after one of the leaders – Praise-God Barebones.
- Cromwell soon found that some of these new MPs had very extreme views, which he did not like. These included getting rid of tithes (a sort of tax) and changing the law so that theft was no longer punishable by death.
- A number of the moderate MPs voted to end Parliament.

The Instrument of Government

- A new Parliament with a new constitution, known as the Instrument of Government, was set up. It said that only godly and religious men could become Members of Parliament.
- In 1653, Cromwell became head of the government for life, called Lord Protector.

Oliver Cromwell

- Cromwell was now in charge of the country and still retained the support of a strong army.

The Council of State

- The Council of State had been appointed following the execution of the King in 1649. Its function was to implement domestic and foreign policy, and ensure the security of the country.
- The Council of State became an advisory service to Cromwell.
- Between 13 and 21 councillors were elected by Parliament to advise the Protector.
- In reality, Cromwell relied on the army for support and chose his own councillors.

Rule of the Major-Generals

- In spring 1655, Cromwell imposed direct military government in England and Wales.
- Cromwell divided England into military districts ruled by army Major-Generals who answered only to him.
- They were responsible for tax collection, local law enforcement, preventing opposition to Cromwell and imposing Cromwell's strict rules.
- This proved deeply unpopular and was seen as a military dictatorship.
- The rule of the Major-Generals was abandoned early in 1657 when Cromwell was forced to sack them.

Division of Power in the Republic

- The Lord Protector ruled the people with Parliament and the Council of State. It was an elected position, but for life.
- Parliament had 400 members from England and 30 each from Scotland and Ireland. It met every three years.
- The Council of State helped rule and advise the Lord Protector. It contained military and civilian members.
- Men who owned property worth more than £200 could vote. Women could not vote.

> **Key Point**
>
> Men without property were not allowed to vote in the republic.

Quick Test

1. Describe why England became a republic.
2. Explain how the Barebones Parliament was set up.
3. Give two reasons why Cromwell abolished the Barebones Parliament.
4. What powers did the Instrument of Government give to Cromwell?
5. What was the role of the Major-Generals?

The Interregnum 2

You must be able to:

- Describe the restrictions on freedom under Cromwell's rule
- Explain why Cromwell refused the crown in 1657
- Explain why the monarchy was restored.

Restrictions under Cromwell's Rule

- The Puritans believed that if you worked hard, lived a good life and had a good soul you would go to heaven. For them, this meant refraining from many activities they saw as immoral.
- When Cromwell became Lord Protector, he imposed restrictions on certain activities.
  - Theatres were closed and restrictions were placed on ale-houses and pubs.
  - Dancing, bear-baiting and most sports were banned.
  - Festivities at Christmas and Easter were outlawed.
  - Swearing was banned and punishable by a fine (and those who kept swearing could be sent to prison).
- Cromwell became unpopular and people became frustrated with the strict rules. Cromwell and his MPs also raised taxes and were seen as greedy.

> ### Key Point
>
> In the Puritan period, Sunday was a very special day, a day to reflect on religion rather than indulge yourself.

Cromwell is Offered the Crown

- By 1657, it was clear that stability was required because too many changes in the style of government had taken place and were proving unpopular. Many remembered the stability of having a king but did not want the Stuarts on the throne.
- In February 1657, Parliament offered the crown to Cromwell.
- He was attracted by the stability of a monarchy, but he had helped to destroy it. He agonised for six weeks, but refused.
- Cromwell had been one of the leaders in executing Charles I, and his supporters could not forget how long and hard they had fought for him. He was also concerned that people would question his motives and suggest he had secretly longed to be king.
- In a ceremony in June 1657, which was very similar to a coronation, Cromwell was re-installed as Lord Protector. He sat on Edward's throne, which had been specially moved from Westminster Abbey. Symbols such as a sword of justice and a sceptre were used.
- From 1657 onwards, Cromwell's health began to decline. It was not clear what would happen to England when Cromwell died.
- It was decided that his son, Richard, would inherit the title. Cromwell died in September 1658. Richard took over, but it was clear he was not good enough for the job. He lacked the full

> ### Key Point
>
> As Lord Protector, Cromwell was now able to choose his own successor.

Statue of Oliver Cromwell

support of the army and Parliament. In 1659, Richard resigned and a senior army officer, General Monck, brought his army to London.

- The Long Parliament, the original Parliament from 1640, which contained many supporters of the monarchy, was recalled by Monck and his army.
- It was clear that this Parliament wanted to restore the monarchy.

Restoration of the Monarchy

- Having fled to Europe following defeat to Cromwell in 1651, Charles II was asked to return to England to become king in 1660.
- Charles told Parliament that he was prepared to show mercy to those who had opposed his father. However, he also ordered that Cromwell's body should be dug up and put on trial as a traitor for the execution of Charles I. Cromwell's body was found guilty and hung from the gallows at Tyburn. His head was removed and displayed in London. Thirteen of those involved in Charles I's execution were also hanged.
- Royal supporters whose land had been confiscated under Cromwell's rule had it restored. The House of Lords and Church of England were both restored; Acts of Parliament made other types of church services illegal and stopped anyone who was not a member of the Church of England from becoming an MP, teacher or priest.
- Charles II was greeted with huge enthusiasm on his return to the country. Many people had disliked Cromwell's harsh rule.
- Charles II was a popular king and loved the ceremony of the position. He was nicknamed the Merry Monarch for his love of parties, wine and horse racing.

Trade with Africa and America

- During this period, England was starting to get rich through its trade with the colonies, especially sugar from the West Indies, grown by slaves.
- In 1661, the Barbados Parliament passed 'An Act for the Better Ordering and Governing of Negroes' in relation to the use of slaves. The act described black people as 'an heathenish, brutish and an uncertaine, dangerous kinde of people' and decreed that slaves were to be treated as property, not people. This act was the basis for other slave trade laws in English colonies.

> **Quick Test**
>
> 1. Give three examples of activities Cromwell banned.
> 2. Describe why Cromwell was becoming unpopular by 1657.
> 3. Why did Cromwell refuse the crown in 1657?
> 4. Why did Cromwell's son Richard fail in the role of Lord Protector?
> 5. Why was Charles II a popular monarch?

> **Timeline**
>
> **1649** Execution of King Charles: the monarchy is abolished and England becomes a republic.
> **1653** Cromwell and his army march to Parliament and close it down.
> **1653** Cromwell is elected as Lord Protector.
> **1655** Cromwell divides the country into districts and puts army Major-Generals in charge.
> **1655–57** The rule of the Major-Generals is established to stop opposition towards Cromwell and to protect law and order.
> **1657** Cromwell is offered the crown, but refuses. He is given extra powers as Lord Protector.
> **1658** Cromwell dies of ill health.
> **1658** Cromwell's son Richard becomes Lord Protector.
> **1659** Richard resigns as Lord Protector due to lack of support.
> **1660** Charles II returns from Holland and restores the monarchy.

Review Questions

The Norman Conquest

1 What period of history begins with the Norman Conquest?

.... [1]

2 Under the feudal system, who owned all the land in England?

.... [1]

3 Who were the villeins?

.... [1]

4 When did Hereward the Wake lead a rebellion?

.... [1]

5 In what ways did Harold, King of the Saxons, have difficulty keeping his throne in 1066?

In your answer you should:
- Give your opinion on the most important reason.
- Discuss other reasons.
- Use evidence and your own knowledge to support your answer.

Write your answer on a separate sheet of paper. [10]

6 How did William use castles to control England from 1066?

In your answer you should:
- Give your opinion of the most important use of castles.
- Give other reasons why castles helped William control England.
- Use evidence and your own knowledge to support your answer.

Write your answer on a separate sheet of paper. [10]

Christendom and the Crusades

1 In what year was Thomas A'Becket murdered?

.... [1]

2 Constantinople was the capital of which Christian Empire?

.... [1]

3 In England, what were abbots in charge of?

.... [1]

4 Who won a great victory at the Battle of Hattin in 1187?

.... [1]

5 Why were heaven and hell important to people in the Middle Ages?

In your answer you should:
* Outline what you think people understood by the terms 'heaven' and 'hell'.
* Use your knowledge to show why heaven and hell were important to people in the Middle Ages.

Write your answer on a separate sheet of paper. [10]

6 Imagine you are a Christian living in the Middle Ages. Explain why it is important to go on a Crusade.

In your answer you should:
* Use your own knowledge to describe briefly what took place on a Crusade.
* Explain at least three reasons why people went on Crusades.

Write your answer on a separate sheet of paper. [10]

Review Questions

Magna Carta

1 Which part of France did John lose in 1214?

.... [1]

2 Who in England was unaffected by Magna Carta?

.... [1]

3 Under Magna Carta, whose agreement did the King need in order to raise taxes?

.... [1]

4 When was the first Parliament called and by whom?

.... [1]

5 Explain how Magna Carta limited the power of the King.

In your answer you should:
- Write two paragraphs: the first dealing with your opinion of the most important limit on the King's power, and the second dealing with other limits.
- In each case, support your answer with examples from Magna Carta.

Write your answer on a separate sheet of paper. [10]

6 Imagine you are living in the reign of King John. Do you regard him as a good or bad king?

In your answer you should:
- Write two paragraphs: the first giving your opinion of why he could be regarded as a good king, and the second explaining why he could be regarded as a bad king.
- Then give your overall judgement of whether he was, on balance, good or bad.
- Support your answer with facts and figures.

Write your answer on a separate sheet of paper. [10]

The Black Death

1 How was the disease brought to England?

.... [1]

2 What did people use to treat the lumps caused by the disease?

.... [1]

3 Why did many villages disappear between 1350 and 1400?

.... [1]

4 What did the Ordinance of Labour of 1349 try to do?

.... [1]

5 Explain how the Black Death affected life in England in the 100 years after 1350.

In your answer you should:
- Describe the effects of the Black Death.
- Give your opinion as to the most important immediate effects of the Black Death, 1348–1350, and then the most important long-term effects (1350–1450).
- Give your opinion of at least two other effects.
- Use facts and figures to support your answer.

Write your answer on a separate sheet of paper. [10]

6 Imagine you lived in England in 1349. Explain how people's lives were changed by the outbreak of the Black Death.

In your answer you should:
- Describe how the Black Death affected where people lived and worked.
- Explain how it affected individual groups such as foreigners and the Church.
- Use facts and figures to support your answer.

Write your answer on a separate sheet of paper. [10]

Practice Questions

The Peasants' Revolt

1 What led villeins to demand wages?

.... [1]

2 Which two advisers did the peasants believe gave poor advice to Richard II?

.... [1]

3 How long did the Hundred Years War last?

.... [1]

4 Which Kentish priest preached that God had not created rich and poor?

.... [1]

5 Do you think Richard II was a weak king?

In your answer you should:
- Give your opinion of the most important reason.
- Compare your opinion with at least two other reasons.
- Use facts and figures to support your answer.

Write your answer on a separate sheet of paper. [10]

6 Explain the causes of the Peasants' Revolt. Which do you think was the most important?

In your answer you should:
- Give your opinion of the most important cause.
- Compare your opinion with other causes.
- Identify the immediate cause as well as other longer-term factors.

Write your answer on a separate sheet of paper. [10]

Reformation and Counter-Reformation

1 Which Act of Parliament made Henry VIII Supreme Head of the Church in England?

.... [1]

2 How many monasteries had Henry dissolved by 1540?

.... [1]

3 Who did Mary I marry?

.... [1]

4 How many Protestants were burnt at the stake during Mary I's reign?

.... [1]

5 How and why did Henry VIII decide to break with Rome?

In your answer you should:
- Give your opinion of the most important reason.
- Identify and explain other reasons.
- Support your answers with facts and figures.

Write your answer on a separate sheet of paper. [10]

6 Explain how Henry VIII changed the way people practised religion in England.

In your answer you should:
- Give your opinion of the most important change.
- Identify and explain other changes.
- Support your answer with facts and figures.

Write your answer on a separate sheet of paper. [10]

Practice Questions

The English Civil Wars

1. What was 'the eleven years of tyranny'?

   .... [1]

2. What month and year did the English Civil Wars break out?

   .... [1]

3. What was the first major battle of the wars?

   .... [1]

4. Where was Charles I executed?

   .... [1]

5. In your opinion, what was the main cause of the English Civil Wars?

   In your answer you should:
   * Give your opinion of the most important cause.
   * Compare your opinion to at least two other causes.

   Write your answer on a separate sheet of paper.   [10]

6. Explain why the Battle of Naseby is often viewed as the most significant battle in the English Civil Wars.

   In your answer you should:
   * Explain the outcome of this battle.
   * Compare it to at least one other battle.

   Write your answer on a separate sheet of paper.   [10]

The Interregnum

1 Why did England become a republic in 1649?

.... [1]

2 How did the Barebones Parliament get its name?

.... [1]

3 What was the punishment for swearing?

.... [1]

4 What happened to Cromwell's body?

.... [1]

5 In your opinion, was Cromwell a successful leader of the country?

In your answer you should:
- Give at least three reasons why he was or was not.
- Give reasons for why he may have been unpopular.

Write your answer on a separate sheet of paper. [10]

6 Describe what life was like for ordinary people under Cromwell's rule.

In your answer you should:
- Describe at least three negative outcomes for ordinary people.
- Use facts to support your answer.

Write your answer on a separate sheet of paper. [10]

Transatlantic Slave Trade

You must be able to:

- Explain how Europeans justified the slave trade
- Describe the way slaves were captured, transported and sold
- Understand what life was like on a plantation.

Origins of Slavery

- Slavery has been around for thousands of years, with the Roman Empire relying heavily on slave labour.
- In the mid-15th century, the Portuguese explored Africa and captured a small number of Africans to be used as slaves.
- By 1600 the slave trade was thriving, with 80 per cent of captured Africans being sent to the Americas to work on plantations.
- The Americas is what we now know as the USA, South America and the Caribbean.

Slaves captured in Africa

Justification for Slavery

- A large workforce was needed in the Americas. Many Native Americans had caught diseases from the European settlers and died.
- Europeans often saw black people as physiologically different, saying that they had smaller brains but were stronger.
- Europeans often claimed Africa was uncivilised. This was despite a rich culture with brilliant education, architecture and traditions – for example, the university in Timbuktu, West Africa, was renowned for its medical excellence.

Capture

- Many slaves were prisoners of war who were sold to Europeans.
- Some African Chiefs traded their own people in exchange for European gunpowder, cloth and jewellery.
- Black people were paid to capture other Africans.

The Triangular Trade

- European ships brought textiles, rum and manufactured goods to Africa.
- From Africa, slaves were shipped to the Americas.
- From the Americas, sugar, tobacco and cotton were shipped to Europe including Britain.
- These transatlantic slave trade routes were known as the 'Triangular Trade'.

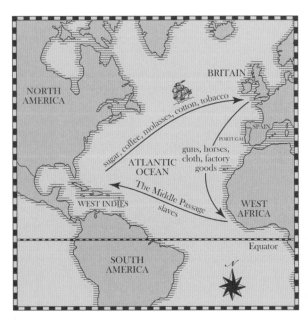

The Triangular Trade

The Middle Passage

- The journey from Africa to the Americas was known as the 'Middle Passage'. It took approximately 12 weeks and was notorious. It was not uncommon for two-thirds of the slaves to die. Conditions were horrific: hundreds of slaves packed together, lying in their own waste. It was rumoured that slave ships could be smelt when miles from port.
- Slaves often tried to overthrow the white sailors, but rarely had much success.
- In 1619, the first group of slaves arrived in Virginia, North America.

> **Key Point**
>
> Between the 15th and 18th centuries at least 12 million African slaves were shipped to the Americas.

Slave Auctions

- Slaves were sold at auction when they arrived in the Americas.
- Many families were separated at slave auctions as they were sold to different owners.
- Slaves were often covered in oil or had their cuts filled with tar to make them look healthier and attract a higher price.
- Young women attracted the highest price as they could produce more slaves. Young men were the next most popular because of their strength.

Former slaves' living quarters on Shirley Plantation, Virginia

Life on the Plantations

- Slave experiences varied depending on their owner, but life was generally very difficult. Slaves worked long hours at strenuous work such as farming cotton or sugar cane.
- Punishments were brutal, and included being whipped or forced to wear a punishment collar, being sold away from your family, and being hanged as an example to other slaves.
- Some slaves managed to escape and formed their own communities. The Maroons of Jamaica were formerly enslaved Africans. Led by 'Nanny of the Maroons', they fought a guerrilla war against the British which ended in 1740 when the British signed a treaty granting them freedom and land.
- Slaves worked hard at keeping their culture alive, holding traditional 'jumping the broom' marriage ceremonies or singing African folk songs.

>
> **Key Point**
>
> There are limited first-hand accounts of the worst plantations because life expectancy was so low.

Sugar cane growing

> **Quick Test**
>
> 1. In the 15th century where was there a university known for medical excellence?
> 2. What is the estimated minimum number of slaves shipped to the Americas?
> 3. What was this journey known as?
> 4. How were slaves sold?
> 5. Name a slave punishment.

Abolition of the Slave Trade

Quick Recall Quiz

You must be able to:

- Describe why there was reluctance to end slavery in both Britain and the USA
- Explain how slavery was abolished in Britain
- Explain the role of the Civil War in ending slavery in America.

Opposition to Abolition in Britain

- When the abolitionists first started to campaign to end slavery in the 18th century they faced lots of opposition in Britain.
- This was because many people directly benefited from slavery. In Liverpool and Bristol, for example, dock workers depended on slavery and many traders like Edward Colston made their fortune trading in slaves.
- Factory owners depended on both the raw materials produced by slaves, and on being able to ship their products to the Caribbean.
- Four of the most prominent anti-slavery campaigners were Thomas Clarkson, Granville Sharp, the MP William Wilberforce and Olaudah Equiano.

Thomas Clarkson

- Thomas Clarkson won a prize for his essay about the horrors of slavery in 1785. He devoted over 60 years of his life to campaigning to end slavery and persuaded William Wilberforce to raise the issue in Parliament.
- He and Granville Sharp founded the Committee for the Abolition of African Slavery.

Granville Sharp

- In addition to his work with Clarkson, Granville Sharp helped achieve the 1772 ruling that ensured slaves could not be forced back to the colonies once they were in Britain.
- He was motivated after befriending Jonathan Strong, a slave who had been badly treated by his owner, and who was at risk of being sold back into slavery.

William Wilberforce

- William Wilberforce raised the issue of the abolition of slavery 18 times in Parliament, despite much early opposition.

Olaudah Equiano

- Olaudah Equiano, an ex-slave who bought his freedom, told of the horrors of slavery in his 1789 autobiography.

Thomas Clarkson

Key Point

The work of the abolitionists changed attitudes and led to a sugar boycott. The 1807 Act was passed by 283 votes to 16.

Olaudah Equiano, an African writer, abolitionist and civil rights campaigner who had formerly been enslaved

Abolition of slavery in the British Empire

- The Slave Trade Abolition Act of 1807 banned the buying and selling of slaves but did not end the use of existing enslaved labour.
- The Slavery Abolition Act of 1833 abolished slavery completely in the British Empire but protecting profit remained a key concern and plantation owners received a share of £20 million in compensation. The slaves received no compensation and were forced into apprenticeship schemes, which tied them to their plantations for up to six years. In reality, little had changed for them.

The American Civil War 1861–65

- For many years the Northern and Southern states of America had been arguing about slavery. The Southern economy was dependent on slavery, largely due to the thriving cotton industry.
- Abraham Lincoln was elected President in 1860. He had spoken out against slavery regularly. Tensions heightened and the American Civil War broke out in 1861.
- The Northern states formed the Union Army and the Southern states formed the Confederate Army.
- Many black people wanted to fight for the Union Army. They were kept separate from white soldiers and paid less.
- Southerners were angry that black soldiers were fighting against them and murdered any they captured.
- Some Northerners began to believe that the war was being fought just for the benefit of black people, which led to lynchings and beatings in some areas.
- Many black people fled or helped the Union Army by building shelters and helping the wounded. Some defended plantations out of loyalty or fear of their masters.
- The Union Army won the war. The thirteenth amendment abolished slavery in the Americas in 1865.

Key Point

In 1948, the United Nations passed a resolution abolishing slavery. Mauritania was the last country to comply in 2007. Of course, slavery still exists illegally in many countries today.

Timeline

1441 Portuguese capture a small group of Africans.

1500–1600 Europeans develop colonies in the Americas.

1619 First group of slaves arrive in North America.

1700s Northern states abolish slavery but it remains important in the South.

1807 The Slave Trade Abolition Act in Britain.

1833 The Slavery Abolition Act in Britain.

1861–65 American Civil War.

1865 Slavery is abolished in the Americas.

Quick Test

1. Who was the ex-slave abolitionist in Britain?
2. Who won a prize for his essay against slavery?
3. What did the 1807 Slave Trade Abolition Act achieve?
4. Who became President of the US in 1860?
5. When was slavery abolished in America?

Britain as the First Industrial Nation 1

You must be able to:

- Understand the factors that caused the Industrial Revolution
- Describe what conditions were like for workers in the cities
- Understand steps taken by some employers to improve life for their workers.

A Period of Rapid Change

- The Industrial Revolution is the title given to the mid-18th to late 19th century in Britain. This was a time of huge change, with mass migration to the towns and cities. In 1750, approximately 20 per cent of people lived in towns and cities; by 1900 this was 75 per cent.
- Previously, the majority of people worked on the land.
- The Industrial Revolution was the result of a combination of factors.
- The population was rising, partly due to improvements in diet and hygiene. The demand for goods rose with it.
- The traditional method of production, the 'Domestic System', where goods were made in the home, was not meeting demand.
- Coal replaced wood as the leading supply of fuel, and provided three times as much energy. It was easy to transport coal as many major mines were near the sea.
- Massive advances in science and technology meant machines were widely produced to be used in factories.
- Railway and canal development further boosted industry.

Change in England's population between 1700 and 1901

1700

Population per square mile

Key:
- less than 100
- from 100 to 260
- over 260

1901

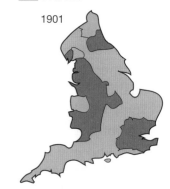

Population per square mile

Key:
- less than 100
- from 100 to 520
- over 520

Development of Factories

- At first, factories were powered by water wheels. This led to Manchester becoming a key industrial city, as fast-running rivers from the Pennines powered industry.
- The textile industry was the first to use this new technology, following Sir Richard Arkwright's invention of the water frame for spinning thread in 1769.
- Eventually, the development of the steam engine and its improvement by James Watt meant industry was not reliant on water power and so the Industrial Revolution could spread further.
- Many industrialists made lots of money. One was George Africanus. Born in West Africa in 1763, he was freed by his owner in England and moved to Nottingham where he married, bought his own house and was thus able to vote.

Sir Richard Arkwright – 'Father of the Industrial Revolution'

Life in the Factories

- While machines would eventually mean a reduction in the amount of workers required, for most of the Industrial Revolution the opposite was true.
- Between 1838 and 1885 the number of workers in the cotton industry doubled to 500 000.
- Life for factory workers was often very tough.
- The development of electricity meant that workers were no longer limited to working solely in daylight.
- Many workers worked 14-hour days.
- Machines lacked safety guards, meaning serious injuries were commonplace.
- Scalping was a particularly nasty accident where the top of the scalp was removed as a worker's hair got caught in the mechanisms.
- Children as young as four were used to crawl under machines to collect thread.
- Punishments were brutal and many people, particularly children, were beaten for not working hard enough.
- Workers sometimes went on strike to fight for better pay, shorter hours and safer working conditions. Some strikes, like that of the London Match Girls in 1888, were successful. Many were not.

A textile mill in Halifax, West Yorkshire

> **Key Point**
>
> The population increase, overcrowding in cities and dangerous conditions in factories reduced life expectancy.

Case Study: Josiah Wedgwood

- Not all industrialists treated their workers terribly.
- Some business owners realised if their workers were treated well their productivity would increase.
- Josiah Wedgwood was a potter from Staffordshire.
- While his factories were still strict, he developed a system for his workers similar to modern sick pay.
- He created schools for his workers' children and hospitals to care for the sick.
- He built a village for his workers to live in that was well maintained.
- In return, Wedgwood expected hard work.

> **Key Point**
>
> Wedgwood wasn't the only factory owner to have these ideas. Other notable examples include Arkwright and the Cadbury family.

> **Quick Test**
>
> 1. Who invented the water frame?
> 2. What percentage of people lived in towns and cities by 1900?
> 3. How many workers were there in the cotton industry by 1885?
> 4. How many hours a day did factory workers usually spend working?
> 5. Which potter tried to improve life for his workers?

Britain as the First Industrial Nation 2

You must be able to:

- Understand the effects of the Industrial Revolution on public health
- Understand the importance of the work of Chadwick and Snow
- Describe the intervention put in place by the government to improve public health.

Public Health in the Industrial Era

- Rapid urbanisation brought with it a decline in living standards.
- Manchester's population increased from 18 000 in 1750 to 303 000 in 1851.
- This left many living in inadequate housing.
- Infectious disease was rife. Between 1800 and 1856, one-third of deaths were from tuberculosis.
- There were four major cholera epidemics in London in the 19th century, with the most serious in 1848.
- Around 50 per cent of those who contracted the disease died. It was most common among the working classes.
- People largely believed that disease was caused by 'miasma', meaning bad air. The true cause of disease was not discovered until Louis Pasteur's Germ Theory was published in 1861.
- Several key individuals became concerned and worked tirelessly to improve public health.

Edwin Chadwick

- In 1832, Edwin Chadwick was appointed assistant commissioner for the Royal Commission Enquiry on the Poor Laws.
- His first major report, published in 1834, led to the Poor Law Amendment Act in the same year.
- This did not go as far as he wanted it to and he became increasingly concerned by the growth of infectious disease.
- His 1842 report, 'The Sanitary Conditions of the Labouring Population', highlighted the extent of the problems.
- This led to the 1848 Public Health Act, which followed a particularly bad cholera epidemic that frightened the government into action.
- This Act encouraged councils to improve sewers, manage refuse collection, appoint a medical officer for every town and improve access to clean water.
- However, it was only a guideline so wasn't strictly enforced and was abolished 10 years later.
- Many people were worried about how much these public health changes would cost, and many people disliked Chadwick, meaning they were less keen to do what he said.

Louis Pasteur

Underground sewers were improved under the 1848 Public Health Act

- Chadwick emphasised that improving the health of the working classes would improve the country as a whole, economically and socially.

John Snow

- John Snow was a doctor who became increasingly concerned about the spread of cholera.
- Controversially, he refused to accept the idea that miasma caused cholera, and explored the idea that it entered the body through the mouth.
- His ideas were published in his 1849 essay 'On the Mode of Communication of Cholera', following the 1848 epidemic.
- In 1854 he made a breakthrough. He identified a water pump in Broad Street in Soho as the source of an outbreak of cholera.
- He could not prove how cholera was caused until the work of Pasteur in the 1860s. However, the pump handle was removed so people couldn't use the water, and the outbreak diminished.

Public Health Act 1875

- Public health continued to be a key issue for debate. Health remained poor among the working classes, and the Public Health Act of 1875 was introduced to address this.
- Many of the Act's terms were similar to the 1848 Act; however this Act's terms were compulsory.
- Local councils were now made to improve water supplies and sewage systems.
- They were also forced to appoint a Medical Health Officer to monitor conditions.
- Measures were introduced to check that food being sold was safe for consumption.
- Shorter working hours were introduced.
- Fines were created for polluting rivers.
- Steps were taken to clear slum housing and improve living standards.
- While progress was gradual, this Act marked a turning point in government attitudes towards public health, and it recognised the work of people such as Chadwick and Snow.

John Snow identified a hand water pump as a source of cholera

Key Point

The Public Health Act of 1875 combined and extended a series of smaller Acts.

Timeline

1769 Richard Arkwright invents water frame.
1769 James Watt improves steam engine.
1830 First passenger railway opens.
1848 Public Health Act.
1853 Smallpox vaccination compulsory.
1854 Improvements in hospital hygiene.
1864 Factory Act – to improve standards and safety measures.
1875 Public Health Act.
1894 Manchester ship canal opens.

Quick Test

1. Which disease accounted for one-third of deaths between 1800 and 1856?
2. Which disease did John Snow study in depth?
3. Why was the Public Health Act of 1848 not successful?
4. What could you be fined for under the Public Health Act of 1875?
5. What were shortened under the Public Health Act of 1875?

Democratic Reform 1

You must be able to:

- Explain how the voting system worked in the 1820s
- Explain why the Reform Act was important
- Understand the demands of the Chartists.

The Voting System in the 1820s

Voting in 1873

- In the 21st century, Britain is a democracy where every adult aged 18 or over is allowed to vote. In the 19th century this was not the case.
- Voting was a privilege for only the wealthiest people in society.
- The country was divided into constituencies called counties and boroughs. Most of these sent two MPs to Parliament.
- Before 1832 the right to vote depended on three things:
  - Gender: Only men over the age of 21 were allowed to vote.
  - Property: In order to vote, an individual had to own property over a certain value.
  - Location: The right to vote varied from borough to borough.
- The system was very unfair. In many areas there was no contest because the local landowner was so influential.
- The local landowner could control the election and guarantee that his candidate would win.
- Bribery and threats of violence were common, and voting was not held in secret.
- The poor, the working classes and women were not represented in Parliament.
- Only men could become MPs. They were not paid a salary, so they had to be very rich to become an MP; Parliament was dominated by rich, aristocratic landowners.
- Rotten boroughs were areas that had a small number of voters who could be bribed easily.
- Dunwich in Suffolk was a rotten borough. It had been destroyed and no longer existed, but the 30 people who used to live there still had the right to vote and could elect two MPs.
- Certain areas of Britain, such as the south of England, could elect more MPs than the north. This is because they were far better represented under the voting system.
- Cities such as Manchester, Sheffield and Leeds had no MPs in the 1820s.
- The rapid population growth in the towns and cities meant there was more chance of new political ideas spreading.
- Reformers believed that Parliament no longer represented the country properly and it needed changing.

Industrial city of Sheffield

The Reform Act 1832

- The first important change to the political system was the 1832 Reform Act. This Act achieved two main things:
  - It extended the franchise so that more men could vote.
  - In an attempt to make the system fairer, it got rid of some of the differences in the system that existed across the country.
- As a result of the Act, rotten boroughs were abolished and some new industrial towns and cities now had their own MPs.
- The effects of this Act were very limited. Still only a tiny percentage of British men could vote in elections (around 25 per cent).

The Chartists

- Chartism was a mass reformist movement that demanded greater change and the vote for all men. It had six key demands:
  - a vote for every man aged 21 and over
  - secret ballots
  - payment for MPs
  - no property qualifications
  - annual Parliaments to put an end to bribery and corruption
  - equal constituencies.
- The movement also demanded an improvement in living conditions, increased wages and the end of workhouses. In 1836, a group of London artisans also formed the London Working Men's Association.
- The Charter was signed by over 1.25 million people but when it was presented to Parliament in 1839, MPs ignored it.
- The Chartists were not the only ones fighting for electoral change. Susanna Inge was Secretary of the London Female Chartist Association from 1842 to 1844. She wanted the vote for all women, something the Chartists couldn't agree to.

The Newport Rising, 1839

- In Newport, Wales, between 5000 and 10000 miners and ironworkers marched on the town, demanding the release of a popular Chartist leader called Henry Vincent.
- Soldiers were brought in to try and stop the demonstration and the leading Chartists were arrested and sentenced to transportation.
- The government believed this showed Chartism was a violent movement and more than 200 Chartists were arrested.

Key Point

Before 1832, the voting system was very unfair. Only men aged 21 and above who owned property could vote.

NOT SO *VERY* UNREASONABLE!!! EH?

Cartoon showing the Charter being presented to Lord Russell

Key Point

The Chartists were a reformist group that demanded change, including the vote for every man over 21 and secret ballots.

Quick Test

1. Who was allowed to vote in the 1820s?
2. Give one reason why the voting system was unfair.
3. What did the 1832 Reform Act try to achieve?
4. How many people signed the Chartist petition presented in 1839?
5. How many people were arrested during the Newport Rising?

Democratic Reform 2

You must be able to:

- Explain why the Chartist movement failed
- Describe how the 1867 Reform Act increased the vote
- Understand how social reform improved people's lives.

The End of Chartism

- In 1848, the Chartists attempted another petition which they said contained 6 million signatures. They planned a mass march to Parliament to deliver the petition. However only 20 000 people turned up and when the petition was inspected it had only 1.9 million signatures. A number of names had even been forged.
- The meeting and petition were a disaster and it would be another 50 years before the demanded changes were made.
- William Cuffey, son of a freed slave, was voted onto the National Executive of the Chartists in 1842. He was sent as a convict to Tasmania for his part in a planned armed uprising in 1848.

Social and Political Reforms after 1867

- The voting system put in place by the 1832 Reform Act remained in 1867, but it had come under increasing pressure from the reformist movements during the 1840s and 1850s.
- By the early 1860s, around 1.5 million men could vote out of a total population of 30 million. However, the lack of secret ballots meant that voters could still be offered bribes or intimidated.
- The system was still unfair and did not give equal representation to all areas of Britain.

Parliamentary Reform Act 1867

- This Reform Act increased the number of men able to vote to almost 2.5 million. MPs believed these better-off working-class men would not demand too much change. The Prime Minister Benjamin Disraeli claimed they were more interested in 'keeping housed, fed and clothed'.
- The Reform Act gave most skilled working-class men in the towns the vote, although the vote was still dominated by the middle class.
- The most important change was that people who rented properties could now vote, which increased the number of voters, particularly in large towns and the new industrial cities.

Prime Minister Benjamin Disraeli

> **Key Point**
>
> The Parliamentary Reform Act increased the number of men who could vote to 2.5 million.

Reforms 1870–71

- In 1870, the government passed the Education Act. This resulted in approximately 3000 to 4000 schools being built for 5–12-year-olds between 1870 and 1880. However, they were not free.
- In 1871, the Bank Holiday Act gave everyone holidays from work by law while the Trade Union Act protected the rights of workers to form a trade union.

Ballot Act 1872

- In 1872, the government introduced the Ballot Act. Voting was now done in secret, in polling booths, in an attempt to deal with the problem of bribery, intimidation and corruption.
- Although this Act failed to end this problem completely, the secret ballot certainly made a difference.

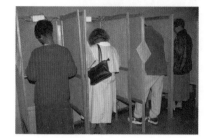

Modern polling booths

Social Reform 1874–75

- The government passed a number of Acts designed to improve working and living conditions for people.
    - The 1874 Factory Act reduced the number of hours people had to work and gave them Saturday afternoon off.
    - In 1875, the government passed the Public Health Act. All towns now had to provide clean water and remove sewage and waste.
    - The Artisans Dwelling Act encouraged local councils to build better quality housing. The Sale of Food and Medicines Act ensured the quality of food and medicines.
- These acts were in part the result of many people pushing for social reform. One of those campaigning was Celestine Edwards. Born in Dominica in 1858, and living in Britain, he campaigned for social reform and an end to racism in the country.

Parliamentary Reform Act 1884

- By the 1880s, it was widely recognised that voters in counties deserved the same political rights as those in the boroughs.
- The 1884 Parliamentary Reform Act created a uniform system across the country under which towns and the countryside were treated the same and each constituency only had one MP.
- The vote was given to most working men in the countryside as well as towns. About two in three men now had the vote, almost 18 per cent of the total population.

> **Key Point**
>
> The 1884 Parliamentary Reform Act increased the number of men who could vote to 6 million.

> **Timeline**
>
> **1820s** Only men aged over 21 with property can vote.
> **1832** Reform Act.
> **1836** London artisans form the London Working Men's Association.
> **1839** Chartist petition.
> **1839** Newport Uprising.
> **1848** End of Chartism.
> **1867** Parliamentary Reform Act increases the number of men who can vote.
> **1872** Ballot Act attempts to end bribery and corruption.
> **1874** Factory Act reduces working hours.
> **1875** Public Health Act provides clean water in towns.

> **Quick Test**
>
> 1. How many signatures did the Chartists really collect in 1848?
> 2. Why was the 1848 petition a disaster?
> 3. How many men could vote following the Reform Act of 1867?
> 4. How many schools were built between 1870 and 1880?
> 5. How did social reform between 1874 and 1875 improve people's lives?

Quick Recall Quiz

Women's Suffrage 1

You must be able to:

- Explain how women were treated in the 19th century
- Describe the role of the Suffragette movement
- Understand the role of the Pankhursts in the Suffragette movement.

Women's Rights in the 19th Century

- In Britain during the 19th century, women were not allowed to vote and many women believed this was unfair.
- It was assumed that women did not need the vote because their husbands made all the important decisions. A woman's role was seen as taking care of the children and the home.
- Women were often treated as second-class citizens, even if they were married. Examples of rules women had to live by include:
  - Everything a woman owned passed to her husband when she married.
  - A woman could be forced to stay in a husband's home against her will.
  - A woman could only divorce her husband if she could prove two of the following: adultery, cruelty or desertion.
- Women saw the right to vote as an important step towards gaining full equality with men. As a result of the Industrial Revolution and the growth of factories and heavy industry, many women were in full-time employment. This meant they now had opportunities to meet in large organised groups to discuss political and social issues.

Women working in a factory

Struggle for Equality

- In 1867, John Stuart Mill tried to amend the Second Reform Act to allow women to vote. Every year from 1870, an MP tried to make a law giving women the vote.
- In 1870 a law was passed that allowed married women to keep their own earnings and in 1882 a further law allowed them to own property; in 1875, women were allowed to stand for election as Guardians of the Poor Law Workhouses.
- This progress had only been made by managing to persuade male members of the Houses of Parliament to pass the laws for them.
- Women were still not allowed to vote or become Members of Parliament.
- 'The Cause' described a movement for women's rights generally. It had no particular political focus.
- In 1872, the National Society for Women's Suffrage was formed. By the end of the 19th century, the issue of gaining the vote had become the focus of women's struggle for equality.

> **Key Point**
>
> In 1903, the women's movement was divided about the best way to protest. Although there were different opinions about methods, they were united in the desire to gain the vote.

The Suffragists – The National Union of Women's Suffrage Societies

- In 1897, various local women's suffrage societies formed the National Union of Women's Suffrage Societies, under the leadership of Millicent Fawcett.
- They wanted the vote for middle-class, property-owning women. They believed the best way to achieve their aims would be to use peaceful tactics such as non-violent demonstrations, petitions and the lobbying of MPs.
- Fawcett believed that if MPs saw the group as intelligent, polite and law-abiding then they would prove that women were responsible enough to gain the vote and participate fully in politics.
- The leadership of the Suffragists was made up of middle-class women but they recognised that in order to have success they also needed to gain the support of working-class women.
- The issue of the vote pulled together women from different sections of society and gave them an identity.
- Millicent Fawcett had to defend her peaceful, non-violent tactics, as a number of women believed that change was taking far too long to arrive.

The Suffragettes – Women's Social and Political Union

- The Women's Social and Political Union was founded by Emmeline Pankhurst and her daughters Christabel and Sylvia in 1903. The Suffragettes were born out of the Suffragist movement.
- Emmeline Pankhurst had been a member of the Manchester Suffragist group but had become angered by the lack of action and slow pace of change.
- The Pankhursts felt that women had waited too long to be given the vote and decided that direct action would be more effective. They believed it was a woman's right to be given the vote.
- They believed it would take an active organisation, with young working-class women, to draw attention to their demands.
- The motto of the Suffragettes was '*Deeds not words*' and from 1912 onwards their campaigning became more violent.
- Law-breaking, violence and hunger strikes were all considered acceptable campaign tactics.

Quick Test

1. For what reasons could women get divorced in the 19th century?
2. What did the law passed in 1870 allow women to do?
3. Who was the leader of the Suffragists?
4. Who founded the Women's Social and Political Union?
5. What was the motto of the Suffragettes?

Millicent Fawcett was the leader of the Suffragist movement

Suffragettes fought for women to be given the vote

Key Point

The Pankhursts believed that direct action was the way to gain more attention for their cause.

Emmeline Pankhurst's portrait on a British stamp

Women's Suffrage 2

Quick Recall Quiz

You must be able to:

- Explain the methods used by the Suffragette movement
- Describe how the Cat and Mouse Act gained sympathy for the Suffragette movement
- Understand how women finally gained the vote.

Actions of the Suffragette Movement

- In 1905 Suffragettes Christabel Pankhurst and Annie Kenney interrupted a meeting in Manchester to ask two politicians, Winston Churchill and Sir Edward Grey, if they believed women should have the right to vote. They then got out a banner that said 'Votes for Women' and shouted at the politicians to answer their questions. Pankhurst and Kenney were thrown out of the meeting and arrested for causing an obstruction and assaulting a police officer.
- In 1906, 30 women went to Downing Street and asked to see the Prime Minister. After banging on the door and demanding to be let in, two of the women tried to rush inside, but were arrested. A third woman was arrested after jumping on the Prime Minister's car and attempting to address the crowd.
- In 1908 a protest rally was held in Hyde Park. Estimates suggest that between 250 000 and 500 000 people attended.
- Sophia Duleep Singh, daughter of the Maharajah of Punjab, goddaughter of Queen Victoria and a close friend of Mrs Pankhurst, was often seen outside Kensington Palace selling *The Suffragette*, much to the embarrassment of King Edward VII.
- In 1909 Marion Wallace Dunlop was sentenced to prison for defacing a wall of St Stephen's Church. She asked to be treated as a political prisoner. This request was denied so she began a hunger strike lasting 91 hours. She was then released from prison.

Poster in support of votes for women

Cat and Mouse Act

- When a Suffragette was sent to prison, it was assumed that she would go on hunger strike as this gained maximum publicity.
- The Cat and Mouse Act allowed the Suffragettes to go on a hunger strike and get weaker and weaker. When they were very weak they were released. Those who were released were so weak that they could take no part in any violence. When they had regained their strength, they were re-arrested and the whole process started again.
- Hunger strikers were force fed by prison doctors using steel mouth clamps and tubes. This was a painful and brutal process.
- Force feeding shocked the public and gained a lot of sympathy for the Suffragettes and their cause.

> **Key Point**
>
> The government's use of the Cat and Mouse Act shocked many people because of its brutality towards women.

Increasing Violence

- In 1911, 220 women were arrested after a series of violent acts that included breaking windows at government offices.
- There were also acts of violence targeted at the Home Office, Treasury and *Daily Mail* newspaper.
- In 1912, Mary Leigh threw a small axe into the Prime Minister's carriage; she also tried to burn down the Theatre Royal. The curtains were set alight, a flaming chair was thrown into the orchestra and a number of small bombs made out of tin cans were set off.
- Leigh was arrested and sentenced to five years in prison.
- In June 1913, Emily Wilding Davison attended the Epsom Derby horse race. As the King's horse was racing past, Emily ran onto the race track and was knocked down by the horse. She suffered a fractured skull and died without regaining consciousness. Her funeral was a huge public spectacle and generated lots of publicity for the Suffragette movement.

Gaining the Vote

- When the First World War broke out many women took on the jobs that had been left by men going off to fight. They proved they could do these jobs just as well as men.
- The Suffragettes used this to publicise the important role that women were playing, even though they disagreed with the war.
- They began to reduce their more violent activities due to the war and its effect on the nation.
- The Suffragists supported the war but saw it as an opportunity to put pressure on the government.
- The government had to introduce a new voting law to allow soldiers and sailors fighting in the war to be able to vote. The Suffragists argued that women should also be included in the new law as they had done so much to help the war effort.
- In 1918, the Representation of the People Act gave women over the age of 30 who owned property the right to vote, and in 1928 the Equal Franchise Act extended this right to include all women.

Key Point

The Suffragette movement suspended many of its more violent actions during the war. It was fearful of a backlash from the public during wartime.

Timeline

1870 and 1882 Laws passed to allow married women to keep income and property.
1872 National Society for Women's Suffrage formed.
1884 Parliamentary Reform Act.
1897 Millicent Fawcett forms the National Union of Women's Suffrage Societies.
1903 Women's Social and Political Union formed by the Pankhursts.
1905 Two members of the Suffragette movement arrested in Manchester.
1906 Protest at Downing Street.
1908 Protest rally in Hyde Park.
1911 220 women arrested for a series of violent protests.
1913 Emily Davison killed by a horse at the Epsom Derby.
1918 Women over 30 who owned property given the right to vote.
1928 All women given the right to vote in Britain.

Quick Test

1. What happened to Christabel Pankhurst and Annie Kenney in 1905?
2. How many people attended the protest rally in Hyde Park?
3. What did Mary Leigh try to do in 1912?
4. How did Emily Wilding Davison die in 1913?
5. In what year were all women given the vote?

The Peasants' Revolt

1 How many peasants were involved in the revolt?

.... [1]

2 What did the rebels do on entering London?

.... [1]

3 Who did the rebels murder?

.... [1]

4 How many rebels were killed?

.... [1]

5 Explain why the Peasants' Revolt failed.

In your answer you should:
- Give your own opinion of the most important reason.
- Identify and explain at least two other reasons.
- Support your answer with facts and figures.

Write your answer on a separate sheet of paper. [10]

6 Explain how you think the Peasants' Revolt changed life in England in the 100 years after 1381.

In your answer you should:
- Give your opinion of the most important change.
- Identify at least two other changes.
- Support your answer with facts and figures.

Write your answer on a separate sheet of paper. [10]

Reformation and Counter-Reformation

1 What was the Pilgrimage of Grace?

.... [1]

2 Which appointments did Henry VIII take over from the Pope?

.... [1]

3 How old was Edward VI when he became King?

.... [1]

4 What did Edward VI remove from churches?

.... [1]

5 Why do you think Henry VIII dissolved (closed) the monasteries?

In your answer you should:
- Give your opinion of the most important reason.
- Support your opinion with facts and figures.
- Compare your choice with other reasons.

Write your answer on a separate sheet of paper. [10]

6 In what ways did religious changes under Edward VI differ from those under Henry VIII?

In your answer you should:
- Give your own opinion of the major difference.
- Identify and explain other differences.
- Support your answer with facts and figures.

Write your answer on a separate sheet of paper. [10]

Review Questions

The English Civil Wars

Write your answers to the following questions on a separate sheet of paper.

1 What was Charles I's wife called? [1]

2 Name an unpopular adviser to Charles I. [1]

3 How many men did each side lose at Edgehill? [1]

4 What was the name of the chief judge at Charles's trial? [1]

5 Study the source below. It shows a painting of Charles's execution from 1649.

What useful information does it give you? What are its drawbacks? [5]

6 In your opinion, how important was the role of Oliver Cromwell in the English Civil Wars?

In your answer you should:
- Assess the importance of his military skill and the development of the New Model Army.
- Evaluate his role in the trial and execution of Charles I. [10]

The Interregnum

Write your answers to the following questions on a separate sheet of paper.

1 What event occurred on 30 January 1649? [1]

2 What was the function of the Council of State? [1]

3 How often did Parliament meet? [1]

4 Who recalled the Long Parliament following Cromwell's death? [1]

5 Describe how the country was governed between 1649 and 1653.

In your answer you should:
- Describe at least three ways that power was divided between different groups.
- Use facts to support your answer. [10]

6 Study the source below, which shows Cromwell and Parliament.

How useful is this for understanding Cromwell's rule during the Interregnum? What are its drawbacks? Give reasons for your answer. [5]

Practice Questions

Transatlantic Slave Trade/Abolition of the Slave Trade

1 Where did 80 per cent of captured Africans get sent to work?

.... [1]

2 What type of slaves usually sold for the most money?

.... [1]

3 When did Britain abolish the slave trade?

.... [1]

4 Between what years did the American Civil War take place?

.... [1]

5 Describe what life was like for a slave from capture to arriving on a plantation.

In your answer you should:
- Give information about how they might have become a slave.
- Provide details about the Middle Passage and slave auctions.

Write your answer on a separate sheet of paper. [10]

Slaves at work on a plantation

6 Who was the most important abolitionist? Explain your answer.

In your answer you should:
- Explain the roles of the abolitionists.
- Give a judgement about the most important.

Write your answer on a separate sheet of paper. [10]

Britain as the First Industrial Nation

1 What became the leading fuel in the industrial era?

_____ [1]

2 Who made an improved steam engine?

_____ [1]

3 There were four epidemics of which disease in 19th-century London?

_____ [1]

4 Which Act was introduced in 1848 and improved upon in 1875?

_____ [1]

5 Describe the reasons for the start of the Industrial Revolution.

In your answer you should:
- Give details of at least three factors contributing to industrialisation in Britain.

Write your answer on a separate sheet of paper. [10]

6 Explain the dangers faced by workers in the cities.

In your answer you should:
- Look at the risks in factories.
- Consider the risks from living conditions.

Write your answer on a separate sheet of paper. [10]

Practice Questions

Democratic Reform

1. In what year did the Reform Act take place?

   .... [1]

2. What was a rotten borough?

   .... [1]

3. How many people were allowed to vote in the early 1860s?

   .... [1]

4. What Act did the government pass in 1872?

   .... [1]

5. In your opinion, why did the voting system need reforming by 1832?

   In your answer you should:
   - Give at least three examples of unfairness in the voting system.
   - Use facts to support your answer.

   Write your answer on a separate sheet of paper. [10]

6. Explain whether the Chartist movement should be viewed as a failure.

   In your answer you should:
   - Explain at least three different negative outcomes for the Chartist movement.
   - Use facts to support your answer.

   Write your answer on a separate sheet of paper. [10]

Women's Suffrage

1 Why were women not allowed to vote?

_____ [1]

2 What changed for women as a result of the law that was passed in 1870?

_____ [1]

3 What year did Marion Wallace Dunlop begin her hunger strike in prison?

_____ [1]

4 Which type of women were given the vote in 1918?

_____ [1]

5 In your opinion, how important was the role of the Pankhursts in the suffrage campaign?

In your answer you should:
- Describe the actions of the Suffragette Movement.
- Take into account other factors involved in the suffrage campaign.
- Use facts to support your answer.

Write your answer on a separate sheet of paper. [10]

6 Explain why the struggle for equality failed in the 19th century.

In your answer you should:
- Give your opinion on at least three different reasons.
- Use facts to support your answer.

Write your answer on a separate sheet of paper. [10]

The First World War 1

You must be able to:

- Explain the causes of the war
- Describe the alliances and opposing forces
- Understand the nature of trench warfare
- Explain why the Gallipoli campaign was a disaster for the Allies.

Quick Recall Quiz

Key Causes of the War

Assassination of Franz Ferdinand

- Archduke Franz Ferdinand was next in line to the Austro-Hungarian throne.
- He was killed on 28 June 1914 by a Serbian extremist, Gavrilo Princip, who was a member of the Black Hand terrorist group.
- Serbians were angry at the treatment of Serbs living in Bosnia, which had been Serbian but was part of Austria-Hungary at this time.
- The assassination led to Austria-Hungary declaring war on Serbia, which triggered a response from Europe's alliance system.

Alliances

- Russia had an agreement to support Serbia should it go to war.
- Germany had an agreement to support Austria-Hungary.
- Britain and France had an agreement to support Russia.
- This meant many countries were drawn into the war.

Arms Race

- There was a long history of rivalry between Britain and Germany.
- Britain had built a powerful new warship called the Dreadnought.
- Germany responded by building their own Dreadnoughts.
- This triggered a competition to have the most powerful navy, known as the arms race. This was important as it made both countries paranoid that the other was preparing for war.

Empires

- Britain had a big empire that Germany was jealous of, causing tension.
- Many European countries were competing to make their empires bigger.

Trench Warfare

- Trench warfare was a recent development. Hundreds of miles of trenches were dug across Europe, with the aim of protecting soldiers from enemy shelling.

Site of Franz Ferdinand's assassination, Sarajevo

A Dreadnought warship

Key Point

War broke out in August 1914. By November 1918, 20 million soldiers were dead.

- Conditions in the trenches were very bad, with rats carrying disease and a condition called trench foot in which soldiers' feet began to rot due to the mud and bacteria.
- Generals struggled to keep up with advances in technology such as machine guns, tanks and poison gas, and many were heavily criticised for their tactics.

An International Response

- Over 1 million Indian troops served during the First World War. Many were rushed to France in 1914 and helped hold the line against the advancing Germans.
- 140 000 workers were provided by the Chinese authorities and employed in a British and French Labour Corps. They performed support work and manual labour such as building dugouts, repairing roads and railways and digging trenches, thus releasing troops for fighting.
- 15 000 men from the Caribbean joined the British West Indies Regiment and served in Europe, the Middle East and Africa.
- Thousands of men from Canada, Australia, New Zealand and the rest of the Empire fought with Britain.

The Gallipoli Campaign

- The Western Front was in stalemate in February 1915.
- Soldiers from Britain and the Empire went to help the Russians who were being threatened by the Turks in the Caucasus.
- The British planned a naval campaign centred around the Gallipoli peninsula in the Dardanelles to divert troops from the Caucasus. The aim was to get Turkey out of the war and to get some of the Balkan states to join the Allies.
- The campaign was a failure. Bad weather meant six British ships were destroyed or damaged before arrival. Heat and disease made conditions difficult for the Allied soldiers.
- The Turks knew the British were on their way and so massively increased their numbers before they arrived.
- In December 1915, the campaign was declared a total failure and abandoned. Troops started to be evacuated. In total, there were more than 250 000 casualties on each side, with some 46 000 Allies killed and 65 000 Turkish soldiers.

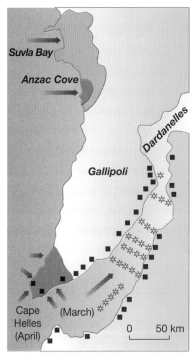

Soldiers in a trench

The Gallipoli campaign

Key:

Ground taken in April

Ground taken in August

■ Turkish forts

✳ Turkish mines

➡ Allied attacks

Quick Test

1. Whose assassination triggered the start of the war?
2. Why were some Serbians angry with Austria-Hungary?
3. What was the name of the new warship?
4. What were the new types of technology used in the war?
5. What factors contributed to Britain failing at Gallipoli?

Key Point

The disaster of Gallipoli contributed to Lloyd George replacing Asquith as Prime Minister in 1916.

The First World War 2

Quick Recall Quiz

You must be able to:

- Describe where the key battles took place
- Explain why historians disagree over the merits of the tactics used on the Western Front
- Understand the consequences of the war.

Battle of Verdun (February–July 1916)

- In February 1916, German General von Falkenhayn decided the key to winning the war was Western France.
- He knew the French would use many soldiers to protect the historically important fortress town of Verdun.
- Falkenhayn believed he could damage the French army.
- However, the French were well led and well prepared.
- Throughout March and April, land near Verdun changed hands many times, with the French led by General Pétain.
- The battle ended in July 1916 as the Allies began the Somme offensive, partly to relieve the French.
- Approximately 400 000 soldiers from each side were killed.
- By October, Verdun and the surrounding area was completely back in French hands and General Pétain was seen as a hero for his role in the campaign.

Battle of the Somme (July–November 1916)

- The Battle of the Somme began in July 1916.
- The first day was the worst ever in British military history with more than 57 000 casualties, including more than 19 000 soldiers killed.
- British General Haig refused to change tactics.
- Men were instructed to walk slowly over 'No Man's Land' resulting in many being killed by German machine guns.
- They were trying to take over a 15-mile stretch of trenches, but by November had advanced only 5 miles.
- Groups of friends fighting in 'Pals Battalions' were wiped out, meaning some communities lost most of their young men.
- In all, there were 500 000 German casualties, 420 000 British and 200 000 French, with over 100 000 British fatalities, 50 000 French and 160 000 German.
- Although the British lost fewer men than the Germans, the battle is seen as disastrous in British military history.

Verdun memorial cemetery

> **Key Point**
>
> No Man's Land was the land between trenches not owned by either side.

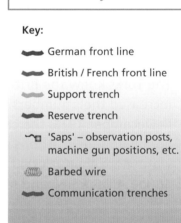

Key:

- German front line
- British / French front line
- Support trench
- Reserve trench
- 'Saps' – observation posts, machine gun positions, etc.
- Barbed wire
- Communication trenches

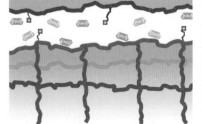

No Man's Land

End of the War

- The war ended on 11 November 1918 when Germany surrendered.
- In all, 8 million soldiers and 9 million civilians had died.

Treaty of Versailles

- A treaty was made on 28 June 1919 to punish Germany for losing the war. It was signed at the Palace of Versailles, just outside Paris, after six months of negotiations.
- Germany was banned from the talks.
- The Treaty angered the German people and was later used as propaganda by extremists in Germany.

Revise

> **Key Point**
>
> Propaganda is information and ideas (true or false) deliberately spread to support a particular group or political view.

Terms of the Treaty

Military Restrictions

- German army to be reduced to 100 000 men.
- No soldiers in Rhineland, the part of Germany next to France. France wanted to make sure Germany could not invade her again.
- No air force.
- No submarines.
- Just six battleships.

Reparations

- Germany to pay £6.6 billion to the Allies for damage caused by the war.

War Guilt Clause (Article 231)

- Germany had to take all the blame for starting the war.

Territorial Losses

- Germany to:
  - give Alsace-Lorraine back to France
  - lose its entire empire
  - give back Upper Silesia to Poland, separating Prussia from the rest of Germany (known as the Polish Corridor)
  - lose important industrial areas such as the Saar where there were many coalfields.

The Rhineland area of Europe

> **Timeline**
>
> **June 1914** Franz Ferdinand assassinated.
> **28 July 1914** War breaks out.
> **Feb–Dec 1915** Gallipoli campaign.
> **1916** Lloyd George becomes Prime Minister.
> **Feb–July 1916** The Battle of Verdun.
> **July–Nov 1916** The Battle of the Somme.
> **11 November 1918** The war ends.
> **28 June 1919** The Treaty of Versailles signed.

Quick Test

1. Who was seen as a hero after Verdun?
2. Who led the British at the Somme?
3. Why did some communities in Britain lose all their young men?
4. How much money did Germany have to pay to the Allies?
5. What is Article 231 often known as?

The Second World War 1

Quick Recall Quiz

You must be able to:

- Explain the causes of the war
- Describe Hitler's aims between 1933 and 1939
- Understand how the treatment of Jews changed between 1933 and 1945.

Hitler's Aims

- Adolf Hitler became Chancellor of Germany in January 1933 and later took on the role of Führer (which means leader). In this role, he operated as a dictator.
- Hitler's aims between 1933 and 1939 were:
  - the reunion of Germany and Austria
  - the cancellation of the Treaty of Versailles
  - rearmament and the return of land taken away by the Treaty of Versailles
  - to destroy Communism
  - to gain land in Russia and Eastern Europe for the German people – *Lebensraum* (living space).

Adolf Hitler

> **Key Point**
>
> Roosevelt became President of the USA in 1933. Like most Americans, he believed in isolationism – it was not America's job to sort out Europe's problems. They would have to do that for themselves.

Rearmament

- From 1933, Hitler began to secretly build up his army and air force. This had been banned by the Treaty of Versailles.
- Britain and France did nothing to prevent this from happening. They were more worried about the power of the Soviet Union.

The Rhineland and Austria

- In 1936, Hitler ordered his troops to march into the Rhineland, which was forbidden by the Treaty of Versailles.
- Many people in Britain and France thought it was reasonable for Germany to have troops protecting its own land.
- In 1938, Hitler sent troops into Austria and forced the Austrian leader to hold a vote on unification.
- Britain, France and Italy had refused to help Austria because they did not want to risk the possibility of war.
- Hitler promised that he wanted peace in Europe.

> **Key Point**
>
> In October 1917, towards the end of the First World War, the communists seized power in Russia. They wanted to make Russia a strong industrial power and, the West thought, to spread communism throughout the world. Some European leaders were more frightened of Russia than of Germany.

The Sudetenland and Czechoslovakia

- In September 1938, Hitler demanded that the Sudetenland area of Czechoslovakia unite with Germany.
- Hitler claimed that people who lived there were German and wanted to unite with Germany.

- Neville Chamberlain, who became British Prime Minister in 1937, visited Hitler three times to attempt to prevent war.
- This policy was known as appeasement. They signed the Munich Pact in 1938. Chamberlain declared that this was 'peace for our time'.
- Chamberlain agreed that Hitler could keep the Sudetenland if he promised not to take over the rest of Czechoslovakia.
- In March 1939, Hitler broke the Munich Pact and German troops invaded the rest of Czechoslovakia.

Poland

- In August 1939, Germany and the Soviet Union signed a non-aggression agreement called the Nazi–Soviet Pact.
- On 1 September 1939, Hitler invaded Poland.
- Britain and France declared war on Germany on 3 September 1939.

Key:
- Germany in 1919
- Territory added to Germany before September 1939
- Remilitarised

German aggression up to September 1939

The Holocaust

- After 1933, the persecution of Jewish people in Germany became commonplace.
- On 9 November 1938, there was a night of violent attacks on Jews and their homes, businesses and synagogues. This is known as *Kristallnacht* (night of broken glass).
- Once the war had begun, the persecution increased. Jews in Germany and occupied countries were rounded up and sent to ghettos. Around 500 000 Polish Jews died of disease and starvation in the ghettos.
- A policy called the 'Final Solution' saw Jews moved into concentration camps, where many died or were executed in gas chambers. The most infamous camps included Auschwitz and Treblinka.
- By the end of the war over 6 million Jewish people had been killed. This is known as the Holocaust.
- Up to 5 million other people were also killed by the Nazis, including Soviet civilians and prisoners of war, Slavic peoples, Romanian gypsies, homosexual men and people with physical or mental disabilities.

> **Key Point**
>
> The policy of appeasement failed because Hitler failed to keep his word and invaded Czechoslovakia and Poland.

The entrance to Auschwitz concentration camp in Poland

Quick Test

1. Why did Britain and France fail to prevent Hitler from rearming?
2. How did Hitler manage to unite Germany and Austria?
3. Why did Hitler demand back the Sudetenland?
4. Why did the policy of appeasement fail?
5. What was the 'Final Solution'?

The Second World War 2

You must be able to:

- Explain why the Battle of Britain was a success
- Describe why Hitler wanted to invade the Soviet Union
- Understand how the war came to an end.

War in Europe

- On 1 September 1939, Germany invaded Poland.
- On 3 September, Britain declared war on Germany.
- By April 1940, Germany had invaded the Netherlands and France. The speed of the German attacks – known as *Blitzkrieg* (lightning war) – took the Allies by surprise.
- British and French troops had been pushed back to the beaches of Dunkirk. They were now trapped between the German army and the English Channel. The only chance of escape was by sea.
- In May 1940, the British government put a plan into action known as Operation Dynamo. The aim was to evacuate 300 000 soldiers by ship from the beaches of Dunkirk. The Royal Navy was used to transport men, and many soldiers were rescued using fishing boats and pleasure steamers.
- Dunkirk is seen as a great success and a plan of courage and resilience. But it also highlighted the power, force and speed of the German army.

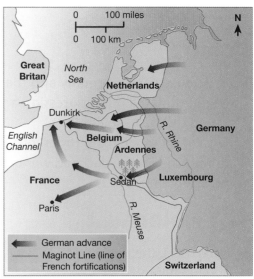

German invasion of France

Battle of Britain, July to October 1940

- After Dunkirk, Hitler controlled all of Western Europe. He then made preparations to invade Britain – Operation Sealion.
- The first task was to use the German air force – the Luftwaffe – to wipe out the British air force – the RAF. If Hitler managed this, he could then send soldiers across the Channel in ships.
- Many people at the time believed in the 'Bomber Theory' – that bombers could get past any air defences and that bombing a country could win the war.
- The Germans believed the Luftwaffe was superior to the RAF.
- In reality, the air forces were evenly matched and Britain had developed a radar system to detect German planes before they reached the English coast.
- British pilots were joined by 574 pilots from around the world to fight off the Luftwaffe. Over half were from Poland and Czechoslovakia, with the rest from across the Empire.
- Although the Germans bombed many airfields, ports and radar stations, they could not defeat the RAF. Hitler called off Operation

> ### Key Point
>
> The early war in Europe demonstrated the strength of the German army. However, the Battle of Britain marked an important turning point as Britain resisted the German attack.

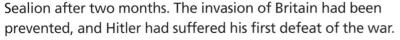

Sealion after two months. The invasion of Britain had been prevented, and Hitler had suffered his first defeat of the war.

- However, Britain was still not safe. Instead, Hitler ordered the Luftwaffe to bomb London and other cities – the Blitz had begun.

War in the East and Battle of Stalingrad

- Hitler wanted to invade the Soviet Union to defeat Communism and gain land for the German people. He believed the Soviets could be defeated in six weeks and ordered an army of 3 million to invade in 1941. However, the Soviets fought fiercely and prevented the Germans advancing and capturing the most important Russian cities of Moscow and Leningrad.
- The harsh Russian winter proved to be a disaster for the Germans. Many German soldiers froze to death as the temperature often dropped to below minus 20°C.
- After the winter, Hitler ordered his troops to capture Stalingrad. It was a brutal battle, but the Soviets gradually took control of Stalingrad and surrounded the German army which was now cut off from its supply chain and forced to surrender.
- This was a turning point in the war as the Soviet army now began to advance towards Germany.

End of the War

- The Germans were fighting on both the Western and Eastern fronts and were rapidly running out of soldiers and supplies.
- The Bomber Campaign had a big impact on Germany, restricting arms production, and destroying many German cities.
- On 6 June 1944, the D-Day invasion took place. Nearly 200 000 British and American soldiers landed in Normandy, northern France, and began advancing through France towards Germany.
- The German army was being pushed further back towards Germany as the British and Americans took control of Western Europe and the Soviets took control of Eastern Europe.
- By 1945 it was clear to Hitler and his army that they were going to be defeated. By April, the British, Americans and Soviets were within days of reaching Berlin and forcing Hitler to surrender. On 30 April 1945, Hitler committed suicide. The war was over. Germany surrendered on 7 May 1945.

> ## Quick Test
>
> 1. What is Blitzkrieg?
> 2. How did the British army escape from Dunkirk?
> 3. What is the name of the German air force?
> 4. How many soldiers did Hitler send to fight Russia?
> 5. How many soldiers landed at Normandy on D-Day?

> **Key Point**
>
> Despite the harsh conditions and extreme brutality of the Battle of Stalingrad, this proved to be a major turning point in the war, as Germany suffered defeat to the Soviet Union.

> **Timeline**
>
> **1933** Hitler becomes Chancellor and subsequently Führer.
> **1936** German troops march into the Rhineland.
> **1938** Austria and Germany unite.
> **1938** Appeasement agreement (Munich Pact).
> **1939** Hitler invades Czechoslovakia and Poland.
> **1939** Britain and France declare war on Germany.
> **1940** Evacuation of Dunkirk.
> **1940** Battle of Britain.
> **1941** Germany invades the Soviet Union.
> **1942** Soviet Union starts to push the German army backwards.
> **1943** German army surrenders at Stalingrad.
> **1944** D-Day landings.
> **1945** Germany surrenders and the war is over.

The Creation of the Welfare State 1

You must be able to:

- Understand the economic, political and social reasons behind the reforms
- Describe the main Liberal reforms
- Explain the successes of these reforms
- Explain the limitations of these reforms.

Background – Need for Reform

- Prior to the 20th century, the government had a 'laissez-faire' approach to welfare. This meant that it didn't believe it was the role of the state to intervene in people's lives.
- The work of social investigators, such as Edwin Chadwick, Charles Booth and Joseph Rowntree, increasingly drew attention to the need for state support for the poor.
- Chadwick had been working in London in the mid-19th century and drew attention to many public health issues, particularly the link between dirty water and cholera.
- Booth was working in London at the end of the 19th century, and discovered 35 per cent of the population there lived below the poverty line.
- The poverty line, or bread line, is the amount of money people need to buy essentials such as food, shelter and basic clothing.
- Seebohm Rowntree built upon the work of his father Joseph. In 1901, he wrote a report showing that 28 per cent of people were living below the poverty line in York.
- In 1899, two-thirds of those signing up to fight in the Boer War were unfit for service.
- Germany had overtaken Britain as an industrial power; it had a strong welfare system for workers.
- The Labour Party was emerging and advertising itself as the 'voice of the working class'. Its manifesto focused heavily on welfare reform.
- The power of trade unions was strengthening, and they demanded better conditions for workers.
- This was a genuine threat to the Liberal government.
- David Lloyd George, Chancellor of the Exchequer from 1906, genuinely wanted to improve the lives of the poor.
- In 1910, however, the Liberal Party did not get a majority and had to form a coalition (a joint government) with Labour.
- Between 1910 and 1912 a series of strikes threatened to bring British industry to a halt, for example the Coal Strike of 1912.

Key Point

The government was not just motivated by sympathy for the poor. It realised there was a large threat to Britain's economic status and national security if the condition of the workers and the army did not improve.

David Lloyd George

Coal mine

Introduction of Reforms

- Seebohm Rowntree highlighted the three times when people were most vulnerable in their lifetime: childhood, old age, and times of unemployment or sickness. The majority of the early reforms were intended to address these issues.

Children's Reforms	Successes	Limitations
1906 Free School Meals Act	Ensured one good meal a day.	Wasn't compulsory, many councils didn't provide them.
1907 School Medical Inspectors Act	Monitored the health of all school children.	There was limited access to health care if there was a problem.

Reforms for the Elderly	Successes	Limitations
1908 Old Age Pensions Act	5s a week for the over 70s or 7s a week for married couples. Fewer people went to the workhouse.	Life expectancy was around 45 for most workers – few people lived to be 70. It was not enough money to live on. You couldn't claim if you had never worked.

Reforms for Workers	Successes	Limitations
1909 Labour Exchanges set up	By 1914 had helped 1 million find work.	Often part-time, temporary or badly paid jobs.
1911 National Insurance Act	Free health care for workers. Paid workers if they were sick or unemployed.	Health care did not extend to the worker's family. The 7s 6d a week it paid out was not enough to support a family. Only paid for a limited time.

Children receiving free school meals today

Workers receiving free health care

Quick Test

1. Who was Chancellor of the Exchequer from 1906?
2. Who wrote a report showing poverty in York?
3. How old did you have to be to claim a pension?
4. When were free school meals introduced?
5. How many people had found work with the Labour Exchanges by 1914?

The Creation of the Welfare State 2

Quick Recall Quiz

You must be able to:

- Understand the impact of the Second World War on welfare reform
- Understand the importance of the Beveridge Report
- Explain the significance of the creation of the NHS
- Outline other welfare reforms that were a result of the Beveridge Report.

Impact of the Second World War

- The Second World War highlighted the need for further welfare measures.
- People had become more accepting of state involvement in their lives. This had been necessary for the war effort with measures such as rationing.
- The evacuation programme had made people aware of the appalling poverty some children were growing up in.
- Health care had become more organised.
- One thousand operating theatres had been opened to cope with the effects of the air raids.
- In addition to this, many temporary hospitals had opened, along with blood transfusion and ambulance services.
- In 1942, the Beveridge Report was published, highlighting the problems Britain faced and outlining solutions.

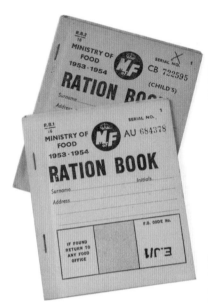

Ration books

Beveridge Report

- William Beveridge was an economist (financial expert) and social reformer.
- He developed a theory of the 'Five Giants of Evil' that Britain needed to overcome if it was to recover from the war.
- He also offered solutions of how this could be achieved.

> **Key Point**
>
> Beveridge published his report in 1942, but his recommendations were not acted upon immediately.

Giant	Problems it was Causing	Solution
Want	Poverty.	Improving National Insurance.
Disease	Unhealthy workforce.	Free health care for all.
Squalor	Unfit living conditions, slum housing.	Social housing.
Ignorance	Inequality in education.	Raising the school leaving age to 15; better school meals.
Idleness	Unemployment.	Work creation schemes to rebuild Britain.

Creation of the NHS

- Aneurin Bevan, Health Minister in the post-war Labour government, set up the National Health Service (NHS) in 1948.
- He intended it to be:
  - Universal: everyone could use it regardless of their circumstances.
  - Comprehensive: to cover all services including dentists and opticians.
  - Free at the point of need: patients would not pay; National Insurance contributions would fund it.
- An ambulance service was to be set up to cover emergencies.

An ambulance today

Opposition to the NHS

- Before he could create the NHS, Bevan had to overcome opposition from doctors.
- Many doctors were worried about losing money, so he agreed to them treating private as well as NHS patients.
- He is said to have 'stuffed their throats with gold' by giving them a high salary.

Key Point

The NHS wasn't the only result of the Beveridge Report. Other important Acts are shown on the timeline.

Problems with the NHS

- It was very expensive; National Insurance didn't cover the costs so it also had to be funded from taxes.
- Certain services soon had to be paid for; for example, prescription charges were introduced in 1951.

Successes of the NHS

- Life expectancy has improved considerably since the NHS was established.
- Many childhood diseases, such as polio, have been eradicated as a result of vaccination programmes.
- It is seen as the 'jewel in the crown' of social reform.

Timeline

1906 Free school meals.
1907 School Medical Inspectors Act.
1908 Children's Charter and old age pensions.
1909 Labour Exchanges set up.
1911 National Insurance Act.
1944 Education Act (implemented 1945); school leaving age raised to 15.
1945 Family allowances introduced.
1946 National Insurance Act extended.
1948 NHS introduced.
1948 National Assistance Act to help those not covered by National Insurance.
1951 Prescription charges introduced.

Quick Test

1. Who spoke about the 'Five Giants of Evil' in his report?
2. Name the 'Five Giants of Evil'.
3. Who was Health Minister when the NHS was created?
4. What was the school leaving age raised to in 1944?
5. What was introduced in 1951?

Britain's Place in the World 1945–Present 1

Quick Recall Quiz

You must be able to:

- Describe how and why the population changed after 1945
- Explain how Britain attempted to rebuild after 1945
- Explain the decline of traditional industries in the post-war period.

Post-war Changes

- Immediately after the Second World War, Britain saw enormous social change. The country was bankrupt after the war.
- The wartime Prime Minister Winston Churchill was voted out. The new Labour government nationalised many industries including electricity, gas, water and health.
- Britain took a long time to recover and food rationing continued until 1954.
- In the 1950s, rebuilding continued. A steady flow of immigrants from Commonwealth nations began, mainly from the Caribbean and the Indian subcontinent.
- In 1956, Britain and France lost control of the Suez Canal during the Suez Crisis. It was clear that Britain was no longer a superpower.
- India and Pakistan had gained their independence in 1947.
- Britain knew it could no longer afford its large empire. By 1970, it had withdrawn from almost all its colonies.

The Suez Canal in Egypt

Population Changes

- Between 1948 and 1997 the population of Britain rose from 47 million to 58 million. The biggest reason for this population increase was more advanced medical care.
- The NHS had been set up in 1948 to provide free health care for everyone.
- Following the Second World War, Britain needed more workers to help rebuild the nation. A campaign encouraged people from the British Commonwealth to move to this country.
- Many people from the West Indies and India moved to Britain. This continued in the 1960s with new immigrants arriving from Asia and Africa.
- During the 1960s, race relations laws made it illegal to discriminate against people because of their nationality or race.
- Emigration from Britain to Australia, New Zealand and South Africa was at its height during the 1970s and 1980s.
- By the 1990s Britain's population was around 58 million and 16 per cent of the population were aged 65 or over.

> **Key Point**
>
> The population rose from 47 million to 58 million between 1948 and 1997.

Britain's population growth

Work Changes

- The world of work has changed a great deal since 1945.
- Traditional industries included coal mining, shipbuilding and steel work.
- These industries have largely disappeared. There is a greater focus now on service industries, banking and finance.
- Between the 1940s and 1990s the number of women in work doubled from 6 million to 12 million.
- In the 1970s, goods made in British factories cost more to produce than importing them from overseas. This meant that a lot of British factories had to close down and unemployment increased.
- Many coal mines closed because the demand for coal in Britain had declined. Electricity was now generated by power stations burning oil or gas from the North Sea.
- In the 1940s, most homes were heated by open coal fires; by the 1980s, most homes had central heating powered by gas, oil or electricity.
- In 1972, coal miners went on strike, leading to huge problems in British working life, including the temporary introduction of a three-day working week, so that electricity could be rationed.
- Recently the huge growth in the use of technology has meant that some jobs have relocated overseas.
- Some companies employ people in countries such as India to work in telephone call centres.
- There are now more self-employed people. In 1979 one in twelve workers were self-employed; by the 1990s this had increased to around one in eight.

Key Point

Many traditional industries such as coal mining, shipbuilding and steel work suffered while there was a growth in service industries, banking and finance.

Oil rig

Workers in an Indian call centre

Quick Test

1. Which industries did Labour nationalise after 1945?
2. What was the population of Britain by 1997?
3. How did immigration help the British economy?
4. How many women were in work by the 1990s?
5. Why did many coal mines close in the 1970s?

Britain's Place in the World 1945–Present 2

Quick Recall Quiz

You must be able to:

- Describe how and why society changed after 1945
- Understand the cultural changes since 1945
- Understand the rise of the teenager and the changing role of women.

Social Change

- There has been huge social and cultural change since the 1940s.
- In the early 1950s few people had a television, and radio was the main form of entertainment. There were plenty of films being made and cinema was very popular.
- Television became more popular following the coronation of the Queen in 1953. Commercial television started in 1955.
- From the 1960s onwards there were huge changes in society.
- Abortion and homosexuality became legal and capital punishment was abolished.
- The contraceptive pill was introduced in the 1960s. At the same time women's roles in society were changing. Many more women could now choose to have a career rather than starting a family and staying at home.
- Young people became known as 'teenagers', and began to break free of parents' control.
- It became acceptable to dress how you wished and listen to new types of music such as rock and roll. British bands such as the Beatles and the Rolling Stones became world famous.
- The voting age was lowered to 18 in 1969.
- By 1963, 82 per cent of all households had a television, 72 per cent a vacuum cleaner, 45 per cent a washing machine and 30 per cent a refrigerator.
- From 1971 to 1983, households having the sole use of a fixed bath or shower rose from 88 per cent to 97 per cent, and those with an indoor toilet from 87 per cent to 97 per cent.
- From 1971 to 1983, the number of households with central heating almost doubled.
- By 1983, 94 per cent of all households had a refrigerator, 81 per cent a colour television, 80 per cent a washing machine, 57 per cent a deep freezer, and 28 per cent a tumble-dryer.
- Popular culture became a lot richer because of the many influences that came from immigration. West Indian and Asian culture became part of British life and Indian and Chinese food changed the options when going out to eat.
- By the beginning of the 21st century, the Internet and social media were changing people's lives.

Key Point

Women and teenagers enjoyed greater freedom and self-expression. Popular culture became a lot richer due to the increase in immigration.

A colour television

A modern washing machine

Political and Economic Change

- Britain emerged from the Second World War as one of the top three superpowers, although in reality a distant third behind the USA and the USSR.
- The 1945 Labour government was largely responsible for what is called the 'post-war consensus'.
- There was a belief that the government should play a positive role in ensuring greater equality in a number of ways.
- The government tried to maintain full employment by cutting taxes and increasing spending.
- There was a growing acceptance that trade unions played an important role in protecting workers' rights.
- The government nationalised industries such as gas, electricity, coal and rail.
- The introduction of the NHS and the Welfare State provided free health care for everyone.
- The British Empire was broken up and transformed into the Commonwealth, an association of independent states.
- Britain joined the North Atlantic Treaty Organisation (NATO) in 1949 and eventually joined the European Community in 1973.
- During the 1960s and 1970s, successive governments attempted to improve the British economy. Britain's economy was often described as the 'sick man of Europe'.
- The 'Winter of Discontent' in 1979 proved that Britain's economy was struggling. There were many strikes in crucial public services.
- The 'Winter of Discontent' turned the public against Labour. The Conservative Party, led by Margaret Thatcher, won the election. She became Britain's first female prime minister.
- During the 1980s, the Conservative government privatised many of the nationalised industries, such as gas, electricity and rail.
- The Conservative government remained in power until 1997 when the Labour Party, led by Tony Blair, won the general election using the slogan 'Things can only get better'.
- The Labour Party remained in power until 2010 when any party failed to gain a majority and a coalition government was formed by the Conservatives and Liberal Democrats.
- Britain's relationship with the US and Europe remained important, particularly around the issue of going to war.
- Brexit (Britain's withdrawal from the EU in 2020) has once again changed Britain's relationship with Europe.

> ## Revise

> ## Key Point
>
> Britain's place in the world diminished as the two superpowers, the USA and the USSR, grew stronger.

Britain's first female prime minister, Margaret Thatcher

> ## Timeline
>
> **1945** Labour responsible for post-war consensus.
> **1948** National Health Service introduced.
> **1949** Britain joins NATO.
> **1955** Commercial television begins.
> **1972** Miners' strike.
> **1973** Britain joins the European Community.
> **1979** The Winter of Discontent leads to Labour losing the general election.
> **1979** Margaret Thatcher becomes Britain's first female prime minister.
> **1991** The Internet becomes available to the public.
> **1997** Labour, led by Tony Blair, wins the general election.

> ## Quick Test
>
> 1. What did the introduction of the pill allow women to do?
> 2. How did young people's lives change during the 1950s/1960s?
> 3. Which two organisations did Britain join and when?
> 4. Why was 1979 known as 'the Winter of Discontent'?
> 5. What was the Labour Party slogan in 1997?

Review Questions

Transatlantic Slave Trade/Abolition of the Slave Trade

Write your answers to the following questions on a separate sheet of paper.

1 What were the transatlantic slave trade routes known as? [1]

2 Which industry thrived in the Southern states of America? [1]

3 What did Thomas Clarkson and Granville Sharp found? [1]

4 What was the name of the army for the Northern states? [1]

5 Study the source below. It is a painting called *The Old Plantation*, painted by a South Carolina plantation owner, John Rose, around 1785.

What can you learn from this source about life for slaves on plantations?
What are its drawbacks? [5]

6 Describe the difficulties faced by slaves on plantations.

In your answer you should:
- Examine the physical hardships faced by slaves.
- Examine the emotional hardships faced by slaves. [10]

Britain as the First Industrial Nation

Write your answers to the following questions on a separate sheet of paper.

1 How many major cholera epidemics were there in 19th-century London? [1]

2 Who devised Germ Theory? [1]

3 How old were some of the youngest factory workers? [1]

4 What happened in 1853? [1]

5 Study the source below about the spread of cholera. It is a political cartoon from 1866, showing death serving cholera to London's children at a water pump.

FUN.—August 18, 1866.

DEATH'S DISPENSARY.

OPEN TO THE POOR, GRATIS, BY PERMISSION OF THE PARISH.

What does the source tell you about public knowledge of cholera in 1866? [5]

6 Explain the importance of Germ Theory.

In your answer you should:
- Explain the problems caused by infectious disease.
- Analyse the acceleration of reforms following Germ Theory.
- Suggest what improvements it made to understanding Snow's work. [10]

Review Questions

Democratic Reform

1 Which three cities had no MPs in the 1820s?

.... [1]

2 How many miners and ironworkers took part in the Newport Rising?

.... [1]

3 Who was Prime Minister in 1867?

.... [1]

4 What did the 1874 Factory Act allow workers to do?

.... [1]

5 In your opinion, why was the 1884 Parliamentary Reform Act an important development?

In your answer you should:
- Give at least two examples of changes to the voting system in 1884.
- Use facts to support your answer.

Write your answer on a separate sheet of paper. [10]

6 Study the source below on the Newport Rising in November 1839.

> A company of soldiers was stationed at the Westgate Hotel. The crowd marched there, loudly cheering. The police fled into the hotel for safety. The soldiers were stationed at the windows, through which some of the crowd fired. The soldiers returned the fire. In about twenty minutes ten of the Chartists were killed on the spot, and fifty others wounded.

What does this source tell you about the Newport Rising that would help you write an account of the event? What are its drawbacks?

Give reasons for your answer.

Write your answer on a separate sheet of paper. [5]

Women's Suffrage

1 In what year did the women's movements start to differ over the methods used?

.... [1]

2 How many women went to Downing Street to protest in 1906?

.... [1]

3 Which three buildings were the main targets of violence in 1911?

.... [1]

4 Why did the government introduce a new voting law during the First World War?

.... [1]

5 Describe how the Cat and Mouse Act gained sympathy for the Suffragette movement.

In your answer you should:
- Explain at least three examples.
- Use facts to support your answer.

Write your answer on a separate sheet of paper.   [10]

6 Study the source below, which is from the Speaker of the House of Commons in 1913.

> The activities of the suffragettes had reached a stage at which nothing was safe from attacks. Churches were burnt, buildings and houses were destroyed, bombs were exploded, the police assaulted and meetings broken up. The feelings in the House hardened opposition to their demands. The result was a defeat of their Bill by 47 votes, which the government had previously promised to support.

Explain why the government failed to support the Suffragette movement.

Write your answer on a separate sheet of paper.   [5]

The First World War

1 In what month and year did the First World War break out?

.... [1]

2 What infection affected soldiers' feet in the trenches?

.... [1]

3 Which general led the French forces at the Battle of Verdun?

.... [1]

4 Where did the main battle between forces from the British Empire and Turkey occur in 1915?

.... [1]

5 In your opinion, what was the main cause of the First World War?

In your answer you should:
* Give your opinion of the most important cause.
* Compare your opinion to at least two other causes.

Write your answer on a separate sheet of paper. [10]

6 Describe why the Battle of the Somme is often viewed as a disaster for the British.

In your answer you should:
* Explain at least three different negative outcomes for the British.
* Use facts and figures to support your answer.

Write your answer on a separate sheet of paper. [10]

The Second World War

1 Why did Hitler want to invade the Rhineland in 1936?

.... [1]

2 How did Neville Chamberlain try to prevent war?

.... [1]

3 What did the Nazi–Soviet Pact agree upon?

.... [1]

4 Why did Hitler want to invade the USSR?

.... [1]

5 Describe the ways in which people were persecuted during the Holocaust.

In your answer you should:
- Give at least three different examples.
- Use facts to support your answer.

Write your answer on a separate sheet of paper. [10]

6 Describe why the Battle of Britain was a success for Britain.

In your answer you should:
- Explain at least three negative outcomes for Hitler.
- Use facts to support your answer.

Write your answer on a separate sheet of paper. [10]

The Creation of the Welfare State

1 Which party emerged as the 'voice of the working class'?

.... [1]

2 Which war highlighted the poor health of possible recruits?

.... [1]

3 A thousand of what were built to deal with the effects of the air raids?

.... [1]

4 When was the NHS established?

.... [1]

5 Explain the reasons for the programme of Liberal welfare reforms.

In your answer you should:
- Give your opinion of the most important cause.
- Give details of at least three motivations for reform.

Write your answer on a separate sheet of paper. [10]

6 How did the war years (1939–45) create a need for new welfare reforms?

In your answer you should:
- Explain the problems highlighted by the war.
- Describe extra services provided because of the war.
- Outline the impact of the Beveridge Report.

Write your answer on a separate sheet of paper. [10]

Britain's Place in the World 1945–Present

1 In what year did food rationing end?

_____ [1]

2 Name three countries British people emigrated to.

_____ [1]

3 In what year did commercial television begin?

_____ [1]

4 What problem occurred due to the 1972 miners' strike?

_____ [1]

5 In your opinion, what is the most important change in Britain since 1945 (for example, social, political, industrial)?

In your answer you should:
* Give your opinion on the most important change.
* Compare your opinions on at least two examples of change.

Write your answer on a separate sheet of paper. [10]

6 Describe why the 1960s changed the lives of women and teenagers.

In your answer you should:
* Describe at least three different positive outcomes.
* Use facts and figures to support your answer.

Write your answer on a separate sheet of paper. [10]

Migration To and From the British Isles 1

Quick Recall Quiz

You must be able to:

- Describe historical trends of immigration to Britain
- Understand why there was mass immigration to Britain after the Second World War
- Explain why immigration legislation arose in the 1960s and 1970s.

Immigration to Britain

- People have come to Britain since the Stone Age. They have come to work, for religious freedom and to escape war.
- In the 3rd century, a group of African men were brought to Britain to guard Hadrian's Wall.
- A Jewish population was recorded in the 12th century.
- By 1770, there were approximately 14000 black people in Britain as a result of the slave trade but few had any real freedom.
- During the First World War, 60000 seamen were drafted in from the British Empire, as well as many soldiers. Some remained in Britain during the interwar years. However, they faced a great deal of prejudice and there were riots against black settlers in 1919.
- Following the Second World War, Britain started to become a more multicultural nation.

> **Key Point**
>
> These are just some examples of minority groups within Britain. There have been many immigrant groups arriving at various points in Britain's history.

After the Second World War

- Many British politicians spoke proudly of Britain's fight against the racism of Nazi Germany and insisted Britain was different.
- At this point, there were relatively few black or Asian people living in Britain.
- Many soldiers from the Commonwealth had fought for Britain during the war.
- The 1948 British Nationality Act gave all 800 million people of the Commonwealth the right to claim British citizenship.
- Immigration from the Commonwealth was not restricted until 1962. From 1955 to 1961, approximately 30 000 people a year were emigrating from the Commonwealth to Britain.

A British passport

Why was Immigration so High?

- The main reason for high immigration after the Second World War was that Britain had a shortage of workers. The NHS had been established in 1948 and desperately needed more workers.
- London Transport looked to the Caribbean to recruit workers.
- Working in Britain was seen as an opportunity to earn a good wage, some of which workers could send back to their families.

- Incentives such as interest-free loans to cover transport costs and the cost of setting up a new home in Britain were offered.

Problems with Immigration

- Racial tensions soon began to develop in communities.
- Highly skilled immigrants were given unskilled jobs.
- Living conditions for immigrants were often cramped.
- Language barriers made it hard for some to find work.
- Newspapers published sensationalist headlines about unclean behaviour and criminal activity among immigrants.
- Young white men sometimes attacked immigrants as there was jealousy over women.

The Notting Hill Riots 1958

- A large Caribbean community settled in Notting Hill.
- Groups of young white men armed themselves with knives and petrol bombs and attacked the black community.
- Over 100 people were arrested.

New Legislation

Law	Details of the Law
Commonwealth Immigration Act 1962	Migrants must have a prearranged job before they could come to Britain and to have been issued with an employment voucher.
The Race Relations Act 1965 and 1968	Discrimination in employment and housing banned. Incitement of racial hatred illegal.
Commonwealth Immigrants Act 1968	As well as an employment voucher, migrants must also have a parent or grandparent in the UK.
Immigration Act 1971	Replaced employment vouchers with 12-month work permits.

> **Key Point**
>
> Immigration remains a controversial and key political issue today.

The annual Notting Hill Carnival takes place to promote cultural unity

> **Quick Test**
>
> 1. Why did the Romans bring Africans to Britain?
> 2. By 1770, how many black people were in the UK?
> 3. Name a company trying to recruit workers after the Second World War.
> 4. What sort of stories did newspapers publish about immigrants?
> 5. Where were there riots in 1958?

Migration To and From the British Isles 2

You must be able to:

- Understand that many people have emigrated from Britain as well as immigrated to it
- Understand why certain groups left Britain
- Explain the problems they faced when arriving in a new country.

Emigration from Britain

- Emigration from Britain is not new.
- The Pilgrim Fathers, groups of Scottish people and many Irish people emigrated as a result of persecution and extreme hardship.

The Pilgrim Fathers

- During the reign of Elizabeth I, England was Protestant.
- However, a small group of Puritans (members of a strict Protestant movement) felt they were being persecuted in England because of their beliefs.
- At first, they left for Holland but remained unhappy there.
- In the summer of 1620, 120 of these Puritans set sail for Virginia where they could set up their own community.
- They were taking a huge risk as they only had a small boat, and others before them had tried and failed to adapt to life in Virginia.
- They faced a difficult journey on their ship, the *Mayflower*, and got blown much further than Virginia.
- They arrived in November, having travelled for three months.
- Most were suffering from scurvy, due to a lack of Vitamin C, by the time they arrived.
- Many of the Native Americans had died by this point, having caught smallpox from previous European settlers.
- The Pilgrim Fathers took food from offerings on Native American graves and used their abandoned homes.
- Some remaining Native Americans attacked them, but were driven away by the Pilgrim Fathers' guns.
- Half of the Pilgrim Fathers died in the first winter. Those who survived did so because they had befriended some of the Native Americans, who helped them build homes and learn to find food in their new environment.
- The end of a successful harvest in 1621 was marked with a special meal, which is what Americans now remember at Thanksgiving.
- More Puritans left England to join this new community. By 1640, 20 000 had arrived and the city of Boston was created.

Key Point

By the end of the 19th century, 5 million Britons lived outside Britain.

A replica of the *Mayflower*

A replica of a settlement created by the Pilgrim Fathers

Key Point

People originally from Britain now live and work all around the world. After World War Two, for example, people could get a passage to Australia or New Zealand for £10 in order to move there and start a new life.

Canadian Scots

- By the 18th century the British Empire was huge, but many parts were of little use because of their small populations.
- The British government sold a large piece of Canadian land, Nova Scotia or 'New Scotland', to two Scottish businessmen.
- They encouraged many Scottish families to go and work for them in 1773.
- The journey was long and difficult. Eighteen children died of dysentery or smallpox on the first ship sent there, *The Hector*.
- When they arrived, the work was hard, but they developed a thriving timber industry which then exported to Britain.
- By the end of the 19th century, there were over 250000 Scottish people in Canada.

The Irish Potato Famine

- In the 19th century there was mass emigration from Ireland, then part of Britain, due to extreme hardship.
- Most Irish farmers were poor and lived off a simple diet with potato being the staple food.
- This led to disaster when, in 1845, the harvest failed due to potato blight.
- By 1849, 1 million people had died, either from starvation or related illnesses.
- Over 4 million Irish people emigrated, mostly to the USA.
- In addition, 150000 settled in England, mainly in Liverpool and Manchester.
- Those who chose to go to America faced a long and expensive journey.
- A ticket was around £200 in today's money and only bought a bed in a cramped cabin with poor facilities.
- Most families struggled to find that money, so often one family member would go and send money back to Ireland.
- Upon arrival in America they faced medical inspections at the notorious Ellis Island.
- Anyone found unfit for work was immediately sent back.
- Life was not easy in America. The Irish migrants often found themselves living in poor tenement blocks and being stigmatised for their Catholic beliefs.

The Nova Scotia flag

 Key Point

In all three case studies, the journey was very difficult.

Ellis Island in New York

 Timeline

1620 Pilgrim Fathers arrive in America.
1773 Scots arrive in Canada.
1840s Many Irish leave for America.
1948 British Nationality Act.
1962 Commonwealth Immigration Act in Britain.
1965 and 1968 Race Relations Act in Britain.
1968 Commonwealth Immigrants Act in Britain.
1971 Immigration Act in Britain.

Quick Test

1. What form of religion did the Pilgrim Fathers practise?
2. What city did they found?
3. Which diseases killed a lot of Scots en route to Canada?
4. What crop failed in Ireland?
5. How much was a ticket to America in the 1840s?

The Kingdom of Benin

Quick Recall Quiz

You must be able to:

- Explain why Benin was so rich and powerful
- Understand why Europeans wanted to visit Benin
- Explain how the kingdom became part of the British Empire in 1897.

Benin's Early Development

- The Kingdom of Benin grew out of the Edo Kingdom, which was made up of a number of villages which were established in the tropical rainforests of West Africa around 900. No one is exactly sure when as most of Benin's early history depends on oral tradition.
- In the 1100s, there were power struggles which led the Edo people to ask a neighbouring king for help. This resulted in the first Oba, or king, of Benin being chosen, Eweka.
- Houses in the kingdom had mud walls and palm leaf roofs, and were grouped around a central courtyard. The city even had streetlights, powered by palm oil. The Royal Palace stood in the centre of the city.
- Benin was situated on all the major trade routes across the Sahara to North Africa and to the coast of West Africa.
- Farming was well developed where the forest had been cleared – people grew yams, cassava, corn, plantain, okra, pepper, gourds, beans and vegetables.
- Under Ewuare the Great (1440–1473), the state expanded into many surrounding areas. Benin City was expanded and a huge wall and ditch were built in his reign. The wall stretched over 16 000 km – only the Great Wall of China is a bigger earthwork.

Early Contact with European Visitors

- Much of the evidence we have about life in Benin comes from the writings and drawings of European visitors.
- In 1472, the Portuguese, whilst exploring the coast of Africa, visited Benin wanting to trade. Cowrie shells and brass manillas (bracelets) were used as currency. The Portuguese wanted slaves too – the Oba supplied around 200 slaves each year.
- The Oba only traded if he thought the terms were good – otherwise he stopped trading. In 1530, he banned the sale of slaves.
- In 1550, the first English traders arrived. They wanted pepper, ivory, palm oil and cloth. In exchange, they brought linen, woollens, iron, copper and glass beads.
- Dutch traders came too. They described a thriving city and busy markets selling all kinds of goods and animals.

Benin City in 1668

Brass manillas were used as currency

Benin Bronzes

- Benin became famous for its bronzes, made using the 'lost-wax' process. Plaques were commissioned by each Oba when he ascended the throne to commemorate his predecessor's reign and were used to decorate the walls of the Royal Palace. They depicted gods and royal figures – they even made bronzes showing European soldiers.
- Europeans thought they were too good to be made by Africans and felt they must have been shown how to do it by Europeans or the Ancient Greeks.
- Craftsmen, organised in guilds just like in Tudor England, also excelled in working with wood and ivory.

A Benin bronze showing the Oba

Impact of Europeans on Benin

- In 1730, Benin again started trading in slaves. Other states were becoming more powerful on profits from slavery, and Benin was getting left behind. They especially wanted guns and ammunition from the Europeans. In 1798, English traders alone bought 20 000 slaves from the Oba.
- Europeans brought Christianity to Benin, and missionaries tried to convert the local people.
- The slave trade led to warfare in the region. Britain banned the slave trade in 1807, and slavery in 1833, but the buying and selling of slaves carried on much longer than that. African powers became less important and the Europeans more powerful in the trade.
- In 1892, the Oba was forced to sign a treaty with Britain, which wanted sole access to trade.

The End of the Kingdom

- In 1897, a British army invaded and destroyed Benin City and made Benin part of the British Empire, during the 'Scramble for Africa'.
- The city was looted and many bronzes and other artefacts were taken back to Britain by the soldiers and sold to museums and galleries.
- There is a growing campaign for the looted bronzes to be returned to Nigeria. In 2022, the Horniman Museum in London announced that it would be returning over 70 artefacts.

Timeline

1170 Eweka becomes Oba.
1440 Ewuare the Great becomes Oba.
1472 First Portuguese traders arrive.
1530 Oba bans the slave trade.
1550 First English traders arrive.
1730 Oba reintroduces slave trade.
1807 Britain bans the slave trade.
1892 Britain forces treaty on Benin.
1897 Britain attacks and destroys Benin, and loots the city.
2018 Campaign to return the Benin Bronzes gathers pace.

Quick Test

1. Where is Benin situated?
2. How long were the walls around the city?
3. How many soldiers could the Oba use in battle in 1450?
4. When did the Oba stop selling slaves?
5. Why did the British capture and destroy Benin City?

Qing China

You must be able to:

- Understand why Qing China was so rich and powerful
- Explain why Europeans wanted to trade with China
- Understand why this eventually led to a clash with the Western powers.

Quick Recall Quiz

Origins of the Chinese Empire

- The first Chinese Empire – the Shang – started around 1700 BCE.
- The emperor had what the Chinese called the 'Mandate of Heaven' – that is, he was appointed to rule by God. But, if he wasn't a good ruler, ruling for the benefit of the people, he could be replaced with a new emperor.
- Beijing has been the capital since 1279 CE, and the Emperor lived in the Forbidden City there. It took 1 million workers 14 years to build.

The Chinese invented many things, including paper (and paper money), gunpowder and fireworks, printing, the compass, the umbrella, kites and mechanical clocks

Qing China

- The Qing Dynasty was established in 1636 but didn't become the imperial dynasty of all of China until 1644.
- Under the Qing emperors, the territory trebled in size and covered virtually the whole area of what we now know as China. Many areas were added following conquest by Emperor Qianlong. The population grew from 150 million to around 450 million people.
- Qing emperors regularly went on tours of inspection all around the country, checking that all was well.
- Qing China was mostly peaceful. Farming prospered, taxes were low. New crops from the Americas (peanuts, sweet potatoes, maize) were introduced, and better strains of rice from South East Asia meant there was plenty to eat and sell.
- The famous Peking Opera first started in Qing China.
- Missionaries, often Jesuits, brought Western-style schools and universities to a few Chinese towns and cities.

When the first Qing emperor came to power, he made all men shave off most of their hair, keeping just a queue or plait as a sign of submission. This 'Lose your hair or lose your head' policy resulted in thousands being executed for refusing to cut their hair.

Blue and White Porcelain

- One of the most famous elements of the Qing dynasty is the blue and white porcelain, which was much in demand in Europe. At its peak, 100 000 craftsmen were employed to make it and in just one year, 1741, an incredible 1.5 million pieces were sent to Europe.
- The porcelain travelled to Europe in the lowest levels of ships because if water got into the hold, it would not harm the cargo. It was almost used as ballast to keep the ships safe.

> **Key Point**
>
> In the 18th century, Qing China became the richest and most powerful country in the world – in 1732, 32 per cent of the world's manufacturing output was made in China.

- Eventually, potteries in Europe like Delft and Royal Worcester learnt how to copy the porcelain and made it themselves.

Trade with the West

- China made lots of money from trade. It exported tea (until the British learnt how to grow it in India), silk, cotton and ceramics. As China didn't want goods from Europe, merchants had to pay for these with silver.
- Only a few ports were allowed to trade with the West – that way the Emperor could control the influence the barbarians had. Canton was the main port – 90 per cent of China's tea was exported through this port.
- In 1793, King George III sent an envoy, Lord Macartney, to meet Emperor Qianlong to ask for the right to trade in more areas. He was refused. Qianlong was aware of England's power, and ordered his officials to build up defences on the coast.
- Much of what we know about China at the time comes from reports made by Macartney and other European visitors.

The End of the Qing Dynasty

- By the 19th century, Qing China was getting weaker. As taxes were low, the Emperor didn't have enough money to keep China strong. A policy of limiting trade with the West meant China was falling behind the new technology of the Industrial Revolution.
- The British started to sell opium to China, against the Emperor's wishes. This led to two 'Opium Wars' in the 1800s, both of which China lost.
- China was forced to open up its trade to the West and grant colonies (Hong Kong was one) to Europeans. Many cities now had concessions – parts of the city where Europeans lived and worked. These were no longer controlled by China.
- A series of wars and rebellions weakened the empire over many years. Poverty, hunger and opposition to corruption finally resulted in a republican revolution in 1911 which forced the abdication of the last emperor, the four-year-old Puyi.

Quick Test

1. When did the Qing Dynasty start?
2. Where was the capital city and where did the emperor live?
3. Through which city did virtually all of China's trade with the West take place?
4. How did the Western Powers pay for their imports from China?
5. What was a 'queue'?

Key Point

In 1793, Emperor Qianlong said: 'Our land is so wealthy and prosperous that we possess all things. Therefore there is no need to exchange the produce of foreign barbarians for our own.'

Key Point

The Chinese called anyone who wasn't Chinese a 'barbarian'.

Timeline

C1700 BCE First Chinese dynasty (the Shang).
1406 Work starts on the Forbidden City.
C16th First Portuguese traders come to China.
1644 Qing Dynasty starts.
1735 Qianlong becomes Emperor.
1793 Lord Macartney arrives to ask Qianlong to increase trade with Britain.
1840 First Opium War.
1856 Second Opium War.
1911 A revolution replaces the Qing Dynasty with a republic.

Mughal India

You must be able to:

- Understand how rich Mughal India was
- Describe how it grew in size and wealth
- Understand why it declined in the 18th century.

Quick Recall Quiz

The Early Mughal Empire

- The Mughal Empire was founded in 1526 by Babur who came from what is now Uzbekistan and conquered much of northern India. Babur's grandson Akbar extended the empire to cover most of the Indian subcontinent. He ruled from 1556–1605 and was probably the most powerful of the Mughal emperors. His empire covered 1500 square miles and 150 million people.
- Most people in India were Hindus. The Mughals were Muslim. Under the Mughals, religious freedom was important. About 15 per cent of the population were Muslims.

A Powerful Empire

- Akbar is said to have had an army of 1 million men. He used cannon and muskets effectively to defeat existing Indian rulers. His cavalry were particularly feared by his enemies.
- Under his rule, roads were built linking the whole country, making trade and control easier.
- His wealth was based on a tax on peasants (50 per cent of their income).

Agriculture

- 80 per cent of the population lived in the countryside making a living from farming. They grew rice and wheat for food, but also as cash crops to pay their taxes. Cotton, mulberries, indigo, opium, pepper and spices were all grown for export.
- Maize and tobacco, crops originally found only in the New World, were widespread in India in the second half of the 17th century and into the 18th.
- Indian farmers used the seed drill long before Jethro Tull invented it in Britain and were better off than farmworkers in England at the time.

Trade with the West

- Columbus sailed across the Atlantic in 1492 in an attempt to open up a sea route to allow Spain to trade with India. Portugal and the Netherlands already traded with the Mughals.

> **Key Point**
>
> The Delhi Sultanate ruled India for 300 years before the Mughals – they too were a powerful state.

The emperor Akbar with his cavalry – a detail from a Mughal painting from around 1590. The court was renowned for its art and culture. You can see lots of Mughal paintings in the V&A Museum.

> **Key Point**
>
> By 1700, Mughal India was the richest country in the world, with 25 per cent of the world's wealth.

- Indian ships were the best in the world – they were sold to European traders who later copied their designs.
- The West could not get enough of Indian silks and textiles and spices. Europe had to pay with silver and gold because apart from woollen cloth (a very small market), they had few goods that the Mughals wanted.

Shah Jahan and the Taj Mahal

- Shah Jahan, the fifth Mughal emperor (from 1628–1658), killed four of his brothers in order to become ruler.
- He had many wives – each time he conquered a new territory, he took one of the leader's relations as a wife. Mumtaz Mahal was his favourite. They had 14 children, although only 7 survived. When she died in 1631, he was heartbroken. He built the Taj Mahal, a mausoleum to house her tomb, opposite his palace where he could see it every day.
- The Taj Mahal was built of red sandstone and covered in white marble. The marble was inlaid with semi-precious stones from China and lapis lazuli from Afghanistan so it would shimmer in the sunlight. It took 20 000 men (and 1 000 elephants) 20 years to build. It is a UNESCO World Heritage Site.

Around 8 million people visit the Taj Mahal each year; other famous Mughal buildings include the Badshahi Mosque and Shalimar Gardens in Lahore and the Fort at Agra

Decline and Fall of the Empire

- All this wealth attracted attention from the West. Robert Fitch was probably the first Englishman to arrive there in 1583. Elizabeth I set up the British East India Company (BEI) to trade with Mughal India – its first expedition went to India in 1608.
- A series of poor emperors weakened the empire – in 1719 alone there were four emperors. Each was killed by rivals. Europeans took advantage of this weakness and began to take control of parts of India. In 1757 the BEI took political control of much of India after its success at the Battle of Palashi, marking the start of the British Raj in India.
- In 1857, the Sepoy Rebellion or Indian Mutiny saw half the Indian Army challenge the BEI, but the rebellion was unsuccessful. The last Mughal Emperor, Bahadur Shah Zafar, was arrested, tried for treason and sent into exile.

Quick Test

1. How many people lived in Mughal India under Babur?
2. How big was Akbar's army?
3. Which people had a higher standard of living – farm workers in India or farm workers in England?
4. When did the first Englishman arrive in India?
5. How did early European traders pay for the goods they bought in India?

Timeline

1492 Columbus sails the Atlantic to try to find a sea route to India.

1526 Babur becomes first Mughal emperor.

1556 Akbar becomes emperor.

1583 Robert Fitch arrives in India.

1608 First British East India Company ship arrives in Surat.

1628 Sha Jahan becomes emperor.

1719 The 'year of four emperors'.

1757 Battle of Palashi.

1857 Sepoy Rebellion or Indian Mutiny; last Mughal emperor is deposed and exiled by the British.

The West Indies: Fighting Back Against Slavery

Quick Recall Quiz

You must be able to:

- Locate the West Indies on a map or in an atlas
- Understand why slavery was so widespread
- Explain the part slaves played in ending slavery.

The West Indies

- Over 7000 islands make up the West Indies. Arawaks and Caribs lived there for many years before Europeans arrived. They had no resistance to European diseases like smallpox and many died when they came into contact with Europeans.
- In 1492, Columbus claimed the West Indies for Spain. English, French, Dutch and Danish colonies were later established in the region and large numbers of plantations were created.
- Pirates used the area to attack Spanish treasure ships sailing to Europe from South America.

The Growth of the Slave Trade

- At first, indentured white labourers and convicted prisoners were used as labour to grow tobacco and cotton on these plantations. Once sugar started to be grown, more labour was needed. The Portuguese had used African slaves to grow sugar on the Atlantic island of Madeira. The idea spread to the West Indies. The first triangular slave trade voyage was made in 1562/63.
- Altogether, 12 million Africans were taken to the Americas as slaves; 5 million to the West Indies.
- The Barbados Slave Code was written in 1661 and provided a legal basis for slavery. In 1643, the population was 18600 whites and 6400 slaves. By 1724 this had become 18400 whites and 55206 slaves. Although the slave code claimed to protect slaves, in practice, they were treated badly.

Resistance to Slavery

- There were many slave revolts – for example, in Guyana, Barbados and Jamaica. All were put down with great severity.
- When the British conquered Jamaica from the Spanish in 1655, many slaves escaped. They fled to the hills and set up camps.
- For many years the British tried and failed to capture the Maroons, as they became known. Finally, in 1740 they made a treaty with them, guaranteeing their freedom if they didn't help other slaves to escape, and if they fought for Britain if the Spanish or French invaded Jamaica.

Key Point

Europeans thought Africans were inferior and savages.

Europeans were afraid of revolts and being killed in their beds and used harsh punishments to deter the slaves

Nanny of the Maroons is a Jamaican hero; she led the guerrilla war against the British

Abolition and the Role of Slaves

- Some slaves managed to get to Britain, often taken there by their owners, and were able to claim freedom as there was no slavery in Britain, as confirmed by the Somerset Case of 1772.
- Ignatius Sancho, for example, was brought to England as a slave at the age of two. He worked as a butler for a philanthropic duke and learnt to read and write before leaving to become a shop owner in London. As a property owner, he was able to vote in the 1774 election – the first black person to do so.
- Olaudah Equiano, an ex-slave from Nigeria, managed to buy his freedom and went on to campaign for an end to slavery. He told of the horrors of slavery in his autobiography, published in 1789. He was a member of the 'Sons of Africa', a group of 12 black men who campaigned for abolition.
- Mary Prince was born in Bermuda to an enslaved African family. She came to London as a servant in 1828 where she wrote her autobiography, the first published account of the life of a black female slave. It was a bestseller and helped to raise awareness of the cruelty of the slave trade. She also wrote to Parliament asking them to free all enslaved people in the Caribbean – the first woman in Britain to petition Parliament.

Sancho spoke out against the slave trade, composed music and wrote extensively; his letters were published after his death and were used to support the movement to end slavery

The Haitian Revolution

- During the French Revolution which began in 1789, many slaves in the French island colony of Saint-Domingue thought they too should be free.
- In 1791, thousands of slaves rose up and attacked their masters. Toussaint L'Ouverture emerged as the leader of the rebels.
- In 1794, the French government officially freed all slaves in its colonies and made them full citizens.
- In 1801, under Napoleon, French forces attacked the island and captured Toussaint, taking him to France where he died.
- The revolution continued and, in 1804, when the French withdrew, Saint-Domingue – or Haiti as it is now called – became the first country in the Caribbean to become independent and the first country to be founded by former slaves.

Timeline

1492 Columbus claims the West Indies for Spain.
1562 The first triangular slave voyage takes place.
1661 Barbados Slave Code is written.
1740 Britain signs a treaty with the Maroons.
1772 Somerset Case.
1774 Ignatius Sancho votes.
1789 French Revolution begins
1791 Toussaint leads a rebellion against the French.
1804 Haiti wins its independence from France.
1807 Britain abolishes the slave trade.
1831 Publication of Mary Prince's autobiography.
1833 Britain abolishes slavery.

Quick Test

1. Why were so many slaves taken to the West Indies?
2. When was the first triangular slave trade voyage?
3. Who were the 'Maroons'?
4. Who was the first black person to vote in an election in England?
5. When did Toussaint L'Ouverture revolt against the French planters?

Review Questions

The First World War

Write your answers to the following questions on a separate sheet of paper.

1 Who assassinated Archduke Franz Ferdinand? [1]

2 How many Allied soldiers died at Gallipoli? [1]

3 What were the trenches aimed at protecting soldiers from? [1]

4 What is Article 231 of the Treaty of Versailles also known as? [1]

5 Study the source below. It is from a German newspaper in 1919. The caption says: 'When we have paid one hundred billion marks then I can give you something to eat.'

„Wart' nur, wenn wir die hundert Milliarden abgeliefert haben, dann gibt es wieder zu essen."

What can you learn from the source about German reactions to the Treaty of Versailles? What are the source's drawbacks? [5]

6 Describe the problems in the trenches.

In your answer you should:
* Explain the problems caused by enemy attack.
* Describe the problems caused by poor conditions. [10]

The Second World War

Write your answers to the following questions on a separate sheet of paper.

1 When did Hitler become Chancellor of Germany? [1]

2 Why did Britain and France refuse to help Austria? [1]

3 What was the code name for the German attempt to invade Britain? [1]

4 How many Jewish people had been killed by the end of the war? [1]

5 In your opinion, what was the most important reason why Germany lost the Second World War?

In your answer you should:
- Explain at least three different reasons.
- Use facts to support your answer. [10]

6 Study the source below, which is from a speech made by Winston Churchill in June 1940.

> The Battle of Britain is about to begin. Upon this battle depends the survival of Christian civilization … The whole fury and might of the enemy must very soon be turned on us. Hitler knows that he will have to break us in this island or lose the war … Let us therefore brace ourselves to our duty, and so bear ourselves that, if the British Empire and its Commonwealth lasts for a thousand years, men will still say, 'This was their finest hour'.

How useful is this source in understanding the importance of the Battle of Britain? What are its drawbacks? [5]

Review Questions

The Creation of the Welfare State

1 What did Chadwick make a link between?

.... [1]

2 Which country was a major industrial power and had a good welfare system at the beginning of the 20th century?

.... [1]

3 In 1908, what was the life expectancy of most workers?

.... [1]

4 Whose throats did Bevan 'stuff with gold'?

.... [1]

5 Study the source below, which is a quote from Dr John Marks, who qualified as a doctor on the day the NHS was established.

> Doctors were a pretty conservative bunch, certainly the older ones, and many hated the NHS. They saw it as the government interfering in the doctor and patient relationship, although some just opposed it outright on political grounds.

What can you learn from this source about why doctors opposed the NHS? What does it not tell you?

Write your answer on a separate sheet of paper. [5]

6 What were the limitations of the programme of Liberal welfare reforms?

In your answer you should:
- Use facts and figures to support your answer.
- Give your opinion about what the main limitations were.

Write your answer on a separate sheet of paper. [10]

Britain's Place in the World 1945–Present

1 In what year did the Suez Crisis take place?

_____ [1]

2 Which two countries were regarded as world superpowers?

_____ [1]

3 Name the two most popular pop music bands in the 1960s.

_____ [1]

4 What percentage of people owned a television by 1963?

_____ [1]

5 Describe the changes in work since 1945.

In your answer you should:
- Give your opinion on the most important changes.
- Compare your opinion on at least two examples of change.

Write your answer on a separate sheet of paper. [10]

6 Describe the reasons why the British population grew between 1948 and 1997.

In your answer you should:
- Explain at least three different outcomes.
- Use facts and figures to support your answer.

Write your answer on a separate sheet of paper. [10]

Practice Questions

Migration To and From the British Isles

Write your answers to the following questions on a separate sheet of paper.

1 How many people did the 1948 British Nationality Act give the right to claim British citizenship? [1]

2 Where did London Transport go to recruit workers in the post-war years? [1]

3 What disease killed a lot of Native Americans? [1]

4 What did many Irish immigrants to America find themselves being stigmatised for? [1]

5 Explain the reasons why immigration to Britain was so high in the post-war years.

In your answer you should:
- Name legislation that allowed this to happen.
- Give details of other incentives/the need for workers. [10]

6 Describe some of the problems following post-war immigration.

In your answer you should mention:
- Race riots.
- Problems immigrants faced. [10]

The Kingdom of Benin

Write your answers to the following questions on a separate sheet of paper.

1 Where does most of our information about the Kingdom of Benin come from? [1]

2 Where in Benin were most of the bronzes on display? [1]

3 Why were Europeans so keen to visit Benin? In your answer you should:
- Give two or three reasons why Europeans went to Benin.
- Say which reason you think was most important.
- Explain how trade with Benin changed over time. [10]

Qing China

Write your answers to the following questions on a separate sheet of paper.

1 How many people lived in Qing China at its peak? [1]

2 What was the 'Mandate of Heaven'? [1]

3 Do you think war between Qing China and the West was inevitable? In your answer you should:
- Give three or four causes of the conflict.
- State which you think was most important.
- Use your own knowledge to support your answer. [10]

Mughal India

Write your answers to the following questions on a separate sheet of paper.

1 By 1700, what percentage of the world's wealth was created by India? [1]

2 When did the Mughal Empire end? [1]

3 Would you agree that religious tolerance was an important part of the success of the Mughal Empire? [10]

The West Indies: Fighting Back Against Slavery

Write your answers to the following questions on a separate sheet of paper.

1 Who led the Maroons in their fight against the British? [1]

2 How many slaves were taken by force to the West Indies? [1]

3 Why did slavery end in the West Indies? In your answer you should:
- Give two or three important causes of abolition.
- Explain which cause you think was most important.
- State why you think the way you do. [10]

Migration To and From the British Isles

Write your answers to the following questions on a separate sheet of paper.

1. When was a Jewish population first recorded in Britain? [1]

2. What was the main occupation of black people in Britain in the 1770s? [1]

3. What did Thanksgiving originally celebrate? [1]

4. What did young white men often accuse black immigrants of doing? [1]

5. Study the source below. It shows racist graffiti in London in the 1950s.

Why does this source **not** give you enough information about the problems black immigrants faced in Britain in the 1950s? [5]

6. Describe immigration to Britain prior to the Second World War.

In your answer you should mention:
- Pre-First World War immigration.
- Immigration as a result of the First World War. [10]

Write your answers to the following questions on a separate sheet of paper.

The Kingdom of Benin

1 When and why did the English first visit Benin? [1]

2 When and why did the Oba decide to restart the trade in slaves? [1]

3 Benin was famous for its bronzes, many of which were stolen by the British in 1897. Some people think the bronzes should be returned. Do you agree? In your answer you should:

- Outline the different views on this topic.
- Explain why people feel so differently about the issue.
- Reach your own conclusion on the issue. [10]

Qing China

4 In 1732, what percentage of the world's manufacturing output was made in China? [1]

5 **a)** Why was the blue porcelain trade so important to China? [4]

b) Why did it end? [2]

Mughal India

6 Who was the greatest Mughal Emperor of all? [1]

7 What were India's main exports to Europe? [1]

8 Who gained the most from trade between Mughal India and Europe? [10]

The West Indies: Fighting Back Against Slavery

9 Why were so many slaves needed in the West Indies? [1]

10 Who was the first freed female slave to publish an autobiography in Britain? [1]

11 Who or what played the biggest part in ending British slavery?

In your answer you should:
- Explain the different factors that contributed to abolition.
- Say what you think was most important. [10]

Mixed Test-Style Questions

Choose just one question to answer. Each question is worth 5 marks.

1 Study the source below on the death of King Harold, King of the Saxons, and answer the question that follows.

It is part of the Bayeux Tapestry, made over 10 years after the Battle of Hastings.

What does this source tell you about the Battle of Hastings that would help you write an account of the battle? What are its drawbacks?

Give reasons for your answer.

2 Study the source below, which was written by a French doctor, Guy de Chauliac, in 1363.

> The particular cause of the disease in each person was the state of the body – bad digestion, weakness or blockage.

Why does this source **not** give you enough information about what people at the time thought caused the Black Death?

Give reasons for your answer.

Mixed Test-Style Questions

Choose just one question to answer. Each question is worth 5 marks.

1 Study the source below, which is a copy of the Chartists' Six Points.

> ## THE SIX POINTS OF THE PEOPLE'S CHARTER.
>
> 1 A VOTE for every man twenty-one years of age, of sound mind, and not undergoing punishment for crime.
> 2 The BALLOT – To protect the elector in the exercise of his vote.
> 3 NO PROPERTY QUALIFICATION for members of Parliament – thus enabling the constituencies to return the man of their choice, be he rich or poor.
> 4 PAYMENT OF MEMBERS, thus enabling an honest tradesman, working man, or other person, to serve a constituency, when taken from his business to attend to the interests of the country.
> 5 EQUAL CONSTITUENCIES, securing the same amount of representation for the same number of electors, instead of allowing small constituencies to swamp the votes of the large ones.
> 6 ANNUAL PARLIAMENT, thus presenting the most effectual check to bribery and intimidation, since though a constituency might be bought once in seven years (even with the ballot), no purse could buy a constituency (under a system of universal suffrage) in each ensuing twelvemonth; and since members, when elected for a year only, would not be able to defy and betray their constituencies as now.

What does this source tell us? Tick true or false.

a) It shows that the Chartists had eight demands. T ☐ F ☐

b) It shows that MPs should be paid to encourage honest men. T ☐ F ☐

c) It shows constituencies were not equally represented. T ☐ F ☐

d) It shows that Chartists demanded the vote for men and women. T ☐ F ☐

e) It shows that the Chartists wanted to end bribery. T ☐ F ☐

2 Study the source below, which is an extract from *Emmeline Pankhurst, My Own Story*, written in 1912.

> What good did all this violent campaigning do us?
>
> For one thing our campaign made women's suffrage a matter of news, it had never been that before. Now the newspapers are full of us.

What useful information does this source give you about women's suffrage? What are its drawbacks?

Give reasons for your answer.

Choose just one question to answer. Each question is worth 5 marks.

1 Study the source below about the dangers of working in the mills.

It is a primary source produced during the Industrial Revolution.

What does this source tell you about dangers in the mills that would help you write an account of working conditions?

Give reasons for your answer.

2 Study the source below, which is from a letter by Private J. Bowles, 2nd/16th Battalion, Queen's Westminster Rifles, in 1916.

> We expect to be relieved tonight but I don't care if we are not because this isn't a bad 'stunt' and I must say I have enjoyed myself immensely. I was off duty at 6pm. We cooked our own grub and lived like lords.

Why does this source **not** give you enough information about what life was like for soldiers fighting in the First World War?

Give reasons for your answer.

Write your answer on a separate sheet of paper.

Choose just one question to answer. Each question is worth 10 marks.

1 Imagine you are a Christian going on a Crusade.

Write an account of why you want to take part in a Crusade.

2 Why do you think King John was forced to sign Magna Carta?

Support your answer with evidence.

3 Give your own opinion as to why the Reformation is seen as an important event in English history.

Support your answer with evidence.

Continue your answer on a separate sheet of paper.

Mixed Test-Style Questions

Choose just one question to answer. Each question is worth 10 marks.

1 Give your own opinion as to why you think the English Civil War was an important event in English history.

Support your answer with evidence.

2 Why do you think Cromwell refused the crown, but agreed to become Lord Protector?

Support your answer with evidence.

3 Imagine you are living in 19th-century Ireland.

Write an account of your life there and your journey to the USA.

_____

_____

_____

_____

_____

_____

_____

_____

_____

_____

_____

_____

Continue your answer on a separate sheet of paper.

Choose just one question to answer. Each question is worth 10 marks.

1 Why did Lloyd George support welfare reform?

Support your answer with evidence.

2 Imagine you are a German soldier who has just fought on the Eastern Front during the Second World War.

Describe your experiences fighting against the Soviets in this brutal conflict.

3 Give your own opinion on why the 1960s is known as 'the Swinging Sixties' and is seen as an important decade in post-war British history.

Support your answer with evidence.

Continue your answer on a separate sheet of paper.

History – Six Key Skills

Chronological understanding

- This is where you try to gain an understanding of dates and the time period you're studying.
- An example could be, what was it like to live in the Middle Ages?

Cultural, ethnic and religious diversity

- This is where you try to understand how different people would have different experiences in the same time period.
- An example could be, how would a landowner's experience of the Peasants' Revolt be different from a peasant's experience?

Change and continuity

- This is where you identify any factors that have changed or continued over a period of time.
- An example could be, how did a king's power change between 1066 and 1660?

Cause and consequence

- This is where you try to explain the reasons for an event happening and the impact the event has.
- An example could be, what were the reasons (causes) for the First World War and what was its impact (consequences)?

Significance

- This is where you try to explain why something is important.
- An example could be, why was the Industrial Revolution so important (significant) to Britain?

Interpretation

- This is when you try to explain why some people think differently about the same event.
- An example could be, why might a Norman think differently about the Norman Conquest compared to a Saxon?

Key Point

The more often you include these skills in your work, the better your work will be and the quicker you will progress!

Answers

Mark Scheme A

Marks are awarded as follows:

Simple, fragmentary answer: **1–2 marks**

Fuller answer with more description: **3–4 marks**

Full description with partial explanation: **5–6 marks**

Full description and explanation, supported by some evidence: **7–8 marks**

Full explanation and description, fully supported by evidence: **9–10 marks**

Pages 4–5 Review Questions

KS2 Key Concepts

1. The correct order is C, A, E, B, D (Iron Age hill forts were built in Britain in 550 BCE; the Roman invasion of Britain by Claudius was in 43 CE; Boudicca's uprising against the Romans was in 61 CE; Augustine's mission that set up Christianity in Britain was in 597 CE; Alfred the Great ruled England from 871 CE to 899 CE) **[5]**

2. Julius Caesar was a **Roman** general. He invaded Britain in 55 BCE, which stands for **Before** the Common Era. Alfred the Great was an **Anglo-Saxon** king. He created peace between the Vikings and the English.

   St Cuthbert was a Christian monk. He brought Christianity to northern England. He built a big monastery on an island off the east coast of northern England called **Lindisfarne**. **[5]**

3. There is no one right answer to this question; you can select any individual but you must give a reason. For example: Julius Caesar because he was powerful enough to invade England; Alfred the Great because he secured peace and order between the Vikings and the English; St Cuthbert, because he spread Christianity throughout the country. **[2]**

4. There is no one right answer to this question; you can select any individual but you must give a reason. For example, Julius Caesar because although he invaded Britain, lots of other individuals did too; Alfred the Great because he did not bring anything to Britain; St Cuthbert because he only spread Christianity in the northern part of England. **[2]**

5. a. Conditions were poor – dangerous, scary, worrying, cruel, violent. **[3]**

   b. Source A talks about the negative points of working in a factory **[1]**, while Source B talks about the positive aspects of working in a factory **[1]**. For example, Source A mentions the dangers such as loss of fingers **[1]** while Source B describes some good things the children received such as education **[1]**. [2 marks for an understanding of both sources, plus 2 marks for an example from both sources.]

   c. One mark for each of the following, up to a maximum of 3 marks: To get more people to work in his factory; to make sure his factory didn't get closed down; to make sure he kept receiving money; to show how conditions had improved after the 1833 Factory Act. **[3]**

6. a. They have labels and are carrying suitcases and bags. **[2]**

   b. i. Mothers would be upset and lonely because it meant splitting up their family. **[2]**

   ii. Children would be upset, lonely, and/or excited. They would miss their family and might forget their parents. **[2]**

   iii. There would be lots of adults and no children. Schools might close down. **[2]**

Pages 6–21 Revise Questions

Page 7 Quick Test: The Norman Conquest 1
1. 1066
2. Harold
3. Edward the Confessor
4. Bayeux Tapestry
5. The feudal system

Page 9 Quick Test: The Norman Conquest 2
1. Northern, south-western and eastern England (the Fens)
2. Hereward the Wake
3. A motte
4. Domesday Book
5. 1087

Page 11 Quick Test: Christendom and the Crusades 1
1. The Pope
2. The Archbishop of Canterbury
3. Monks, nuns, abbots, abbesses and friars
4. You were no longer a member of the Catholic Church and were damned according to the Catholic authorities
5. To help them get into heaven

Page 13 Quick Test: Christendom and the Crusades 2
1. Thomas A'Becket
2. 1170
3. To escape punishment
4. A Muslim warrior and king
5. King Richard I

Page 15 Quick Test: Magna Carta 1
1. John soft sword
2. Stephen Langton
3. Stopped marriages and burials in England and excommunicated him
4. Took money from the Church and expelled monks from England
5. Great Charter

Page 17 Quick Test: Magna Carta 2

1. 1215
2. Runnymede
3. £100
4. Barons and bishops
5. Knights and townspeople

Page 19 Quick Test: The Black Death 1

1. 1348–50
2. Via black rats that came by boat from Europe
3. From fleas that lived on rats
4. 25 million
5. Toads and leeches

Page 21 Quick Test: The Black Death 2

1. Flu symptoms, sweating, coughing, lumps on arms and legs (first red, then black), high temperature, blotches
2. Five days
3. Jewish people
4. Food prices rose
5. Villeins were given more food and money for working the land

Pages 22–25 Practice Questions

Page 22 The Norman Conquest

1. Germany [1]
2. Normandy [1]
3. Harald Hardrada [1]
4. An outer area around Norman castles containing housing and surrounded by a fence [1]

For questions 5 and 6, see Mark Scheme A.

5. Your answer should include the following reasons, backed up with explanations and facts:
   * William was a relation of the Saxon king, Edward the Confessor.
   * Harold, King of the Saxons, was proclaimed English king on the death of Edward the Confessor.
   * William was one of a number of foreign monarchs who could claim the English throne.
6. A good answer would include the following reasons:
   * The Saxons had already fought at Stamford Bridge and would therefore have been tired.
   * The Saxon's king, Harold, had been killed meaning they did not have a leader.
   * William's army did not have as far to walk so they were in better fighting spirit than the Saxons.

Page 23 Christendom and the Crusades

1. Emperor of Byzantium [1]
2. Canterbury [1]
3. Jerusalem [1]
4. A journey to a religious place [1]

For questions 5 and 6 see Mark Scheme A.

5. There is no right answer to this question and you need to use your imagination. You might include the following points:
   * You cannot read or write so you look to Church leaders, like priests, for guidance and help.

* Monasteries provide you with shelter and food when going on a pilgrimage and offer help when you are sick or orphaned.
* You believe life on earth is short, after you die you will go to heaven or hell, and religion can help you get to heaven.

6. Here are some of the differences you might mention in your answer:
   * Priests were educated and could read and write. They looked after a parish of people, usually in a village. They worked among ordinary people and conducted daily religious services for them.
   * Monks lived in monasteries separate from ordinary people. They did not conduct religious services for ordinary people, but they performed a variety of functions such as praying for people to get to heaven and looking after the sick, elderly and needy.

Page 24 Magna Carta

1. 1215 [1]
2. The powers of the English king [1]
3. Trial by a jury of fellow Englishmen [1]
4. Excommunicated him [1]

For questions 5 and 6 see Mark Scheme A.

5. A good answer would make the following points:
   * John was not a warrior like his predecessor, his elder brother, Richard the Lionheart.
   * John lost lands in France.
   * He quarrelled with the Pope and the Church.
   * He fought and lost a war with the barons.
   * John was forced to sign Magna Carta.
6. A good answer would include the following reasons:
   * John had lost wars in France.
   * He conducted costly wars in Ireland and Scotland, which cost the barons money.
   * John did not consult the barons in the running of the country.
   * John had a major quarrel with the Church and the Pope, which affected the barons.

Page 25 The Black Death

1. 7 500 [1]
2. The lumps on the body turned black [1]
3. Roughly every 10 years [1]
4. Due to a labour shortage, they were offered more money and land to work the lord's land [1]

For questions 5 and 6 see Mark Scheme A.

5. A good answer would include the following:
   * Description of two symptoms such as sweating, coughing, buboes, high temperatures or blotches.
   * Explanation of the problems these would cause.
   * The Black Death usually led to the victims dying within five days.
6. A good answer would include some of the following methods:
   * By praying and punishing themselves because they believed the Black Death had been sent by God.

- Blaming and attacking foreigners for bringing the disease to England.
- Moving out of towns and places where the Black Death occurred.
- Using a variety of remedies to stop them contracting the disease, such as herbs, flowers, fire and animals.

Pages 26–41 Revise Questions

Page 27 Quick Test: The Peasants' Revolt 1
1. Introduction of the Poll Tax in 1380
2. Essex and Kent (counties close to London)
3. 10 years old
4. Five pence
5. Fobbing

Page 29 Quick Test: The Peasants' Revolt 2
1. Wat Tyler
2. Mile End
3. Ending the Poll Tax, freedom for all, and that the poor should receive the Church's wealth
4. Ending the Poll Tax
5. Rioting

Page 31 Quick Test: Reformation and Counter-Reformation 1
1. Latin
2. Germany
3. Because he did not have a son and Catherine was too old to have any more children
4. Anne Boleyn
5. 1536

Page 33 Quick Test: Reformation and Counter-Reformation 2
1. 1539
2. Edward Seymour
3. English
4. The bread and wine were symbolic and did not actually become the body and blood of Jesus
5. She put to death many of the Catholic Church's opponents

Page 35 Quick Test: The English Civil Wars 1
1. She was Catholic
2. A new prayer book
3. His nephew Prince Rupert
4. The Battle of Edgehill
5. The Battle of Marston Moor

Page 37 Quick Test: The English Civil Wars 2
1. The New Model Army
2. Bristol
3. The Scots
4. He only chose those he knew wanted the King to stand trial
5. 30 January 1649

Page 39 Quick Test: The Interregnum 1
1. The King had been executed
2. Oliver Cromwell selected 140 Puritans to become MPs
3. Its MPs had extreme views; they wanted to change the theft law; they wanted to get rid of tithes
4. Executive powers as Lord Protector
5. They were responsible for tax collection, law enforcement, and preventing opposition

Page 41 Quick Test: The Interregnum 2
1. Theatres, pubs, dancing, bear-baiting, sports, Christmas and Easter, swearing
2. He had imposed strict rules and raised taxes
3. He was concerned that people would question his motives
4. He did not have the support of the army and Parliament
5. He got rid of the Puritans' harsh laws

Pages 42–45 Review Questions

Page 42 The Norman Conquest
1. Middle Ages [1]
2. The king [1]
3. Farm labourers or peasants who had to work several days each year for their lord in return for small plots of land [1]
4. In the decade after 1066 [1]

For questions 5 and 6 see Mark Scheme A.
5. Your answer should include the following difficulties faced by Harold, backed up with full explanations:
   - He had to march his army to Yorkshire to fight Harald Hardrada, King of Norway and Denmark, in the north of England in 1066.
   - He then had to march his army all the way to Sussex to fight William of Normandy shortly afterwards.
6. Your answer should include the following ways in which castles helped William control England, backed up with explanations and facts:
   - Castles became local centres of military power.
   - They allowed the Normans to control England.
   - Castles were a symbol of Norman power.

Page 43 Christendom and the Crusades
1. 1170 [1]
2. Byzantium [1]
3. Monasteries [1]
4. Salah u Din, also known as Saladin [1]

For questions 5 and 6 see Mark Scheme A.
5. A good answer might make the following points:
   - People were very religious in the Middle Ages.
   - It was believed that good people who did good things would have eternal life in heaven.
   - Those who behaved badly on earth would face eternal pain and suffering in hell.
6. Your answer must link back to religious reasons. A good answer would fully describe and explain the following:
   - To capture Jerusalem because it was of religious importance.
   - To enter into heaven.
   - To increase the power of the Church.

Page 44 Magna Carta
1. Poitou [1]
2. Villeins (those not freemen) [1]
3. The barons and bishops [1]
4. In 1265 by Simon de Montfort [1]

For questions 5 and 6 see Mark Scheme A.

5. A good answer would include the following:
   - The King had to consult the barons.
   - The King eventually had to call a Parliament in order to raise taxes.
   - The King had limited power in his dealings with the Church.
   - Freemen now had the right to trial by jury.

6. There is no right answer to this question; you need to use your imagination. Some points you might make are:
   - John had a major quarrel with the Pope and Church, which meant religious services were withdrawn and churches shut down.
   - John lost lots of land in France.
   - John fought costly wars in Ireland and against Scotland.
   - John gave freemen rights under Magna Carta.
   - Many of John's problems were caused by the barons.

Page 45 The Black Death
1. By black rats on boats coming from Europe [1]
2. Figs, butter and raw onions [1]
3. The populations had declined so severely [1]
4. Tried to keep wages at pre-Black Death levels [1]

For questions 5 and 6 see Mark Scheme A.

5. A good answer would cover the following points, backed up with evidence and full explanations:
   - Villages were abandoned.
   - There was a shortage of labour.
   - Many people began to lose faith in religion.
   - It helped create the conditions for the Peasants' Revolt.

6. There is no right answer to this question; you need to use your imagination. Try to capture the fear and panic that the Black Death caused. You might include some of the following issues:
   - Fear that the end of the world was coming.
   - Fear that the Black Death was a punishment from God.
   - The need to flee areas affected by the disease, leaving behind your source of work.
   - If you were a foreigner you might be blamed and attacked for bringing the disease to England.

Pages 46–49 Practice Questions

Page 46 The Peasants' Revolt
1. A shortage of villeins [1]
2. Simon of Sudbury and Robert Hales [1]
3. 116 years [1]
4. John Ball [1]

For questions 5 and 6 see Mark Scheme A.

5. Whatever your opinion, a good answer would include some of the following considerations:
   - Richard II was very young and had to rely on others to help him make decisions.
   - He inherited a costly war with France.
   - He unwisely introduced the Poll Tax, which treated rich and poor alike.

- He helped cause the Peasants' Revolt.

6. A good answer would include the following causes:
   - The Black Death had led to a major drop in the population and villeins no longer wanted to work without wages.
   - The Poll Tax treated rich and poor alike and this was resented by the poor.
   - Richard II was fighting a very costly war with France for which he kept raising taxes.
   - Peasants believed Richard II was badly advised and wanted an end to the Poll Tax.
   A judgement on the most important cause should be reached.

Page 47 Reformation and Counter-Reformation
1. The Act of Supremacy 1534 [1]
2. Over 800 [1]
3. Philip of Spain [1]
4. Over 200 [1]

For questions 5 and 6 see Mark Scheme A.

5. A good answer would fully describe and explain the following:
   - Henry VIII wanted to divorce Catherine of Aragon. The Pope refused to allow this so he had to break with Rome.
   - Henry VIII wanted more wealth, which he wanted to take from the Church.
   - Henry VIII wanted more power. By being Head of the Church he became very powerful.
   - Ideas about forming a Christian Church outside the Catholic Church were gaining popularity in England at the time of Henry VIII's reign.

6. A good answer would fully describe and explain the following:
   - Henry VIII was now seen as Head of the Church, not the Pope.
   - Religious services were in English instead of Latin.
   - Bibles in English were placed in every church.
   - Church services were made simpler.

Page 48 The English Civil Wars
1. The years 1629–40 when Charles I ruled without Parliament [1]
2. August 1642 [1]
3. The Battle of Edgehill [1]
4. Outside the Banqueting Hall in London [1]

For questions 5 and 6 see Mark Scheme A.

5. Your answer should give an opinion and compare it to two others. Possible causes are:
   - Religion
   - Power
   - Money.

6. Your answer might include the following reasons, with the best answers making comparisons to other battles.
   - After this battle it became clear the Royalists would lose the war.
   - Cromwell rose to lead the Parliamentarians during this battle.

- This battle was a decisive victory, unlike Edgehill where no one won.

Page 49 The Interregnum

1. The King had been executed by Parliament [1]
2. Named after one of the leaders of Parliament, Praise-God Barebones [1]
3. A fine or prison [1]
4. His body was put on trial and hung at Tyburn, and his head was removed [1]

For questions 5 and 6 see Mark Scheme A.

5. Your answer should give an opinion and at least three examples. Examples may include:
   - Cromwell became Lord Protector. He retained the support of a strong army and was popular. He attempted to introduce a fair method of sharing power. He tried to ensure that the country was religious.
   - Royalists accused him of being responsible for the execution of the King. He imposed strict laws and rules on the country, which many people disliked. He had to use the army to run the country.
6. Your answer might include the following reasons, giving three different negative outcomes and backed up with facts.
   - Strict rules were introduced and many activities were banned for being immoral.
   - Cromwell imposed military government on the people of England with the rule of the Major-Generals.
   - Cromwell raised taxes and was seen as being greedy.
   - He was accused of having the King executed for his own personal gain.

Pages 50–65 Revise Questions

Page 51 Quick Test: Transatlantic Slave Trade

1. Timbuktu
2. 12 million
3. The Middle Passage
4. At auction
5. Whipped; forced to wear a punishment collar; sold away from your family; hanged

Page 53 Quick Test: Abolition of the Slave Trade

1. Olaudah Equiano
2. Thomas Clarkson
3. It banned the buying and selling of slaves
4. Abraham Lincoln
5. 1865

Page 55 Quick Test: Britain as the First Industrial Nation 1

1. Arkwright
2. 75 per cent
3. 500000
4. 14 hours
5. Josiah Wedgwood

Page 57 Quick Test: Britain as the First Industrial Nation 2

1. Tuberculosis
2. Cholera
3. It was only a guideline, wasn't strictly enforced and was abolished 10 years later

4. Polluting rivers
5. Working hours

Page 59 Quick Test: Democratic Reform 1

1. Men over 21 with property
2. Bribery
3. An extension of the franchise and a fairer system by removing regional differences
4. 1.25 million
5. More than 200

Page 61 Quick Test: Democratic Reform 2

1. 1.9 million
2. It contained forged signatures
3. 2.5 million
4. Between 3000 and 4000
5. Living and working conditions got better

Page 63 Quick Test: Women's Suffrage 1

1. Adultery, cruelty or desertion
2. Keep their own earnings after marriage
3. Millicent Fawcett
4. Emmeline Pankhurst and her daughters Christabel and Sylvia
5. 'Deeds not words'

Page 65 Quick Test: Women's Suffrage 2

1. They were arrested after interrupting a political meeting
2. 250000 to 500000
3. Throw an axe into the Prime Minister's carriage and burn down the Theatre Royal
4. She was knocked down by the King's horse
5. 1928

Pages 66–69 Review Questions

Page 66 The Peasants' Revolt

1. Between 50000 and 60000 [1]
2. Attacked the homes of the King's advisers [1]
3. The Bishop of London, the Royal Treasurer, and John Legge, organiser of the Poll Tax [1]
4. 1500 [1]

For questions 5 and 6 see Mark Scheme A.

5. A good answer would fully describe and explain the following:
   - The peasants were mainly from only Essex and Kent, not the whole country.
   - Their leader, Wat Tyler, was killed by the Mayor of London.
   - Richard II promised to give the peasants what they wanted.
   - The King used the army to crush the rebels.
   - Richard II reneged on his promises.
   - The peasants were poorly armed.
6. A good answer would fully describe and explain the following:
   - The Poll Tax was withdrawn.
   - Eventually villeinage came to an end and all Englishmen were freemen.

- The King still ruled, without giving in to the peasants' demands.
- Lords were forced to pay their peasants wages.

Page 67 Reformation and Counter-Reformation
1. A rebellion against Henry in the north of England [1]
2. Appointment of the Archbishop of Canterbury and the bishops [1]
3. Nine years old [1]
4. Religious statues and paintings [1]

For questions 5 and 6 see Mark Scheme A.

5. A good answer would fully cover the following reasons:
   - Many monks were no longer performing their duties properly.
   - Henry VIII wanted to own monastic lands, to increase his wealth.
   - Henry and his advisers no longer believed monks played a useful part in religion.
   - Henry wanted to increase his own power at the expense of the Church by taking more land.
6. A good answer would fully describe and explain the following differences:
   - Henry VIII had kept most Catholic religious services.
   - Edward VI changed how churches were organised: the altar was replaced by a table, church walls were whitewashed, statues and paintings were removed.
   - Edward VI introduced the Book of Common Prayer, containing new religious services.
   - Edward VI dissolved (closed) the last remaining monasteries, completing the work of Henry VIII.

Page 68 The English Civil Wars
1. Henrietta Maria [1]
2. William Laud [1]
3. 1500 [1]
4. John Bradshaw [1]
5. **One mark** for each valid observation (**5 marks** maximum). You might include the following observations:
   - It shows people fainting in shock.
   - It conveys that there was a large crowd/it was an important event.
   - You can see a boy trying to catch the King's blood.
   - A drawback is that it doesn't tell us what happened after the execution.
   - Another drawback is that it is mainly from the point of view of the crowd rather than Cromwell.

For question 6 see Mark Scheme A.

6. Your answer might include the following points, with the best answers looking at both sides of the argument.
   - Drew at Edgehill but won at Marston Moor before he was really important.
   - At Naseby his New Model Army crushed the King and gained a decisive victory.
   - Cromwell signed Charles's death warrant.

Page 69 The Interregnum
1. Execution of Charles I [1]
2. Its role was to implement domestic and foreign policy [1]
3. Every three years [1]
4. General Monck's army [1]

For question 5 see Mark Scheme A.

5. Your answer might include the following examples, backed up with facts:
   - England became a republic and Parliament ruled the country.
   - The Barebones Parliament contained 140 Puritans.
   - The Council of State contained army and civilian members.
   - The army was strong and remained loyal to Oliver Cromwell.
6. **One mark** for each valid observation (**5 marks** maximum). You might include the following observations:
   - It shows Cromwell accepting the role of Lord Protector.
   - Cromwell needed the support of the army.
   - Some MPs look angry because they are shaking their fists.
   - A drawback is that it doesn't explain why Cromwell is being offered the role of Lord Protector.

Pages 70–73 Practice Questions

Page 70 Transatlantic Slave Trade/Abolition of the Slave Trade
1. The Americas [1]
2. Young women [1]
3. 1807 [1]
4. 1861–65 [1]

For questions 5 and 6 see Mark Scheme A.

5. Your answer should give details about capture, the Middle Passage and auctions. Possible detail includes:
   - Chiefs/paid Africans were often used to capture slaves.
   - Conditions on the Middle Passage were horrific and sometimes two-thirds of slaves died onboard.
   - Many families were separated at slave auctions.
6. Your answer should give details about the role of at least three abolitionists and reach a judgement about which was the most important. Possible detail includes:
   - Olaudah Equiano had first-hand experience of being a slave.
   - Wilberforce raised the issue in Parliament 18 times.
   - Clarkson devoted 60 years of his life to ending slavery.

Page 71 Britain as the First Industrial Nation
1. Coal [1]
2. James Watt [1]
3. Cholera [1]
4. The Public Health Act [1]

For questions 5 and 6 see Mark Scheme A.

5. Your answer should detail at least three factors contributing to industrialisation. These could include:
   - Old methods of production were not meeting demand.
   - A rising population led to a rising demand for goods.
   - Improvements in science and technology.
6. Your answer should consider a variety of dangers. These could include:
   - Information about dangers in the factories, e.g. scalping, long working hours, punishments.

- Details about workers' living conditions.
- Information about epidemics and infectious disease, e.g. cholera and TB.

Page 72 Democratic Reform

1. 1832 [1]
2. An area that had a small number of voters who could be bribed easily [1]
3. 1.5 million men [1]
4. Ballot Act [1]

For questions 5 and 6 see Mark Scheme A.

5. Your answer should explain at least three examples of unfairness. Examples may include:
   - The power and influence of local landowners.
   - Bribery and threats of violence, because voting was not secret.
   - Industrial towns and cities such as Manchester having no MPs.
   - Ordinary, working-class people and women not being represented in Parliament.
6. Your answer might include the following reasons, giving three different negative outcomes and backed up with facts and figures:
   - Parliament ignoring Chartist petitions, despite being signed by 1.25 million people.
   - Violent disturbances leading to arrest and imprisonment of Chartist leaders.
   - Forging signatures on petitions.
   - Lack of support for marches and the failure to win their six key demands.

Page 73 Women's Suffrage

1. It was assumed that husbands made all the important decisions [1]
2. They were allowed to keep income and property after marriage [1]
3. 1909 [1]
4. Women aged 30 or over who owned property [1]

For questions 5 and 6 see Mark Scheme A.

5. Your answer should give an opinion and at least three reasons. Examples of the importance of the Pankhursts are:
   - Women's Social and Political Union founded by Emmeline, Christabel and Sylvia in 1903.
   - Their motto was 'Deeds not words' and they believed in direct action.
   - Law breaking, violence and hunger strikes were all acceptable campaign methods.
   - They disrupted a meeting in Manchester in 1905 and demanded the right to vote.
6. Your answer might include the following reasons, giving three different negative outcomes and backed up with facts.
   - Women were often treated poorly, even if they were married.
   - Women could not become MPs or vote.

- There was no particular political focus for the campaigns.
- The Suffragists were only set up in 1897, and believed in peaceful tactics.

Pages 74–89 Revise Questions

Page 75 Quick Test: The First World War 1

1. Archduke Franz Ferdinand
2. Because of the poor treatment of Serbians living in Bosnia
3. Dreadnought
4. Machine guns, tanks and poison gas
5. Heat and disease

Page 77 Quick Test: The First World War 2

1. General Pétain
2. General Haig
3. Pals Battalions, where groups of men from the same area fought together, were wiped out
4. £6.6 billion
5. War Guilt Clause

Page 79 Quick Test: The Second World War 1

1. It was done secretly; Britain and France were more concerned with the Soviet Union
2. He invaded the country and forced a fixed vote
3. He claimed people living there were German and wanted union with Germany
4. Hitler ignored it
5. The moving of Jews to concentration camps

Page 81 Quick Test: The Second World War 2

1. Lightning war (speedy)
2. From the beach by boat
3. Luftwaffe
4. 3 million
5. 200 000

Page 83 Quick Test: The Creation of the Welfare State 1

1. David Lloyd George
2. Seebohm Rowntree
3. 70
4. 1906
5. 1 million

Page 85 Quick Test: The Creation of the Welfare State 2

1. Beveridge
2. Want, Disease, Squalor, Ignorance, Idleness
3. Aneurin Bevan
4. 15
5. Prescription charges

Page 87 Quick Test: Britain's Place in the World 1945–Present 1

1. Electricity, gas, water and health
2. 58 million
3. By rebuilding it after the war
4. 12 million
5. Demand had declined because homes now used gas, oil or electricity

Page 89 Quick Test: Britain's Place in the World 1945–Present 2

1. Choose when to or whether to have children
2. They had more freedom from their parents' control

3. NATO in 1949, and the European Community in 1973
4. There were lots of public service strikes
5. 'Things can only get better'

Page 90 Transatlantic Slave Trade/Abolition of the Slave Trade

1. The 'Triangular Trade' [1]
2. Cotton [1]
3. The Committee for the Abolition of African Slavery [1]
4. Union Army [1]
5. **One mark** for each valid observation (**5 marks** maximum). You might include the following observations:
   - Musical instruments – preserving cultural identity.
   - Might show jumping the broom tradition.
   - Slaves look well dressed – some slaves were well cared for.
   - A drawback is that it is only an example of one plantation – it is painted by the owner so it might make it look better than it was.
   - It also doesn't show slave punishments.

For question 6 see Mark Scheme A.

6. Your answer might include the following reasons, with the best answers looking at a wide range of points.
   - Punishments such as beatings, lynchings and killings.
   - Trauma such as being sold away from family; having name changed.

Page 91 Britain as the First Industrial Nation

1. Four [1]
2. Louis Pasteur [1]
3. Four years old [1]
4. Smallpox vaccination made compulsory [1]
5. **One mark** for each valid observation (**5 marks** maximum). You might include the following observations:
   - A water pump could be a source of cholera.
   - Cholera was a common cause of death, particularly in children.
   - John Snow's work was recognised after he removed the pump on Broad Street.
   - The poor were most at risk; you can see these children are poor by looking at their clothes.
   - Little had changed by this point; many people were still reliant on dirty water despite Snow's work, as the source shows lots of children collecting water.

For question 6 see Mark Scheme A.

6. Your answer might include the following reasons, with the best answers focusing clearly on importance.
   - Up to this point, incorrect theories such as 'miasma' had been used to explain disease.
   - There had been many epidemics of infectious disease at this time; now it was possible to develop strategies to cure them.
   - It allowed scientists such as Snow to explain their work and find greater acceptance of their findings.

Page 92 Democratic Reform

1. Manchester, Sheffield and Leeds [1]
2. between 5000 and 10000 [1]
3. Benjamin Disraeli [1]
4. Take Saturday afternoon off [1]

For question 5 see Mark Scheme A.

5. Your answer should explain at least two important developments. Examples may include:
   - Two-thirds of men could now vote.
   - The number of voters tripled to 6 million.
   - Voters in different areas were given the same voting rights.
6. **One mark** for each valid observation (**5 marks** maximum.) You might include the following observations:
   - The uprising was popular because the crowd were cheering and enthusiastic.
   - The government thought the situation would become very violent so they brought in the army.
   - There was a high number of casualties.
   - A drawback is that it doesn't explain how the uprising ended, and is only one opinion of the event.

Page 93 Women's Suffrage

1. 1903 [1]
2. 30 [1]
3. Home Office, Treasury and *Daily Mail* offices [1]
4. To allow soldiers and sailors fighting in the war the right to vote [1]

For question 5 see Mark Scheme A.

5. Your answer should give an opinion and at least three reasons. Examples could include:
   - Sending Suffragettes to prison attracted lots of publicity.
   - Women in prison went on hunger strike.
   - Hunger strikers were later force fed by prison doctors.
   - When women were released from prison, they were weak and suffering ill health.
6. **One mark** for each valid observation (**5 marks** maximum). You might include the following observations:
   - They used violence to gain attention.
   - The government believed that the Suffragettes were a danger to society.
   - MPs failed to support the cause because of the increase in violence.
   - The government had promised to support the Suffragettes, but changed their mind in 1913.

Page 94 The First World War

1. July 1914 [1]
2. Trench foot [1]
3. General Pétain [1]
4. Gallipoli [1]

For questions 5 and 6 see Mark Scheme A.

5. Your answer should give an opinion and compare it to two others. Possible causes are:
   - The assassination of Archduke Franz Ferdinand.

- The arms race.
- Empires.
- The alliance system.

6. Your answer might include the following reasons, giving three different negative outcomes and backed up with facts and figures:
   - There were more than 57 000 casualties, including more than 19 000 soldiers killed, on the first day alone.
   - General Haig was heavily criticised for not changing tactics.
   - In five months the British only advanced five miles.

Page 95 The Second World War
1. Hitler claimed German land should be protected by German troops [1]
2. With a policy called Appeasement [1]
3. The USSR and Germany agreed not to fight each other [1]
4. To fight Communism, and for *Lebensraum* [1]

For questions 5 and 6 see Mark Scheme A.
5. Your answer may include the following examples:
   - Initial persecution from 1933 tended to be non-violent.
   - Jewish people lost their businesses and had their freedom restricted.
   - During *Kristallnacht*, many Jewish homes, businesses and synagogues were destroyed, persecution now became openly violent.
   - Jewish people were rounded up and forced into ghettos, many died from disease or starvation.
   - The 'Final Solution' involved the use of gas chambers and death camps.

6. Your answer might include the following reasons, giving three different positive outcomes and backed up with facts.
   - Britain had developed radar technology to detect German aircraft.
   - Britain was not invaded by the German army.
   - It demonstrated the strength of the RAF.
   - Hitler called off Operation Sealion after only two months.

Page 96 The Creation of the Welfare State
1. The Labour Party [1]
2. The Boer War [1]
3. Operating theatres [1]
4. 1948 [1]

For questions 5 and 6 see Mark Scheme A.
5. Your answer should give an opinion and compare it to two others. Possible causes are:
   - The Labour Party was emerging as the 'voice of the working class' and talked of the need for reform.
   - The Boer War had highlighted the poor health of the working class.
   - The work of social investigators showed the need for reform.
   - The genuine charitable motivation of people such as Lloyd George.

6. Your answer might include the following reasons:
   - The Beveridge Report made recommendations based around the Five Giants of Evil.
   - The evacuation programme highlighted child poverty.

- Medical facilities improved to cope with air raids.
- There was a change in attitudes about political involvement in people's lives.

Page 97 Britain's Place in the World 1945–Present
1. 1954 [1]
2. Australia, New Zealand and South Africa [1]
3. 1955 [1]
4. Introduction of a three-day working week and electricity rationing [1]

For questions 5 and 6 see Mark Scheme A.
5. Your answer should give an opinion and compare it to two others. Examples of changes since 1945 may include:
   - Huge population increase from 47 million up to 58 million.
   - Changes in work with the disappearance of traditional industries such as coal mining, shipbuilding and steel.
   - Social changes and increasing ownership of household goods and electrical items.
   - Political change, introduction of the NHS and the government trying to ensure equality for all.

6. Your answer might include the following reasons, giving three different positive outcomes and backed up with facts.
   - Introduction of the contraceptive pill and legalised abortion.
   - The growth of youth culture, including changes in pop music and youth consumerism.
   - Women's changing role in society, and an increase in the number of women in work.
   - Lowering of the voting age to 18.

Pages 98–109 Revise Questions

Page 99 Quick Test: Migration To and From the British Isles 1
1. To guard Hadrian's Wall
2. approximately 14 000
3. NHS; London Transport
4. Sensationalist ones about unclean behaviour and criminal activity
5. Notting Hill

Page 101 Quick Test: Migration To and From the British Isles 2
1. Puritanism
2. Boston
3. Dysentery and smallpox
4. Potatoes
5. £200 in today's money

Page 103 Quick Test: The Kingdom of Benin
1. In the rainforest of West Africa
2. 16 000 kms
3. 100 000
4. 1530
5. To make it part of the British Empire.

Page 105 Quick Test: Qing China
1. 1644 (although power was initially seized in 1636)
2. Beijing was the capital and the emperor lived in the Forbidden City.
3. Canton

4. With silver – and, later, by smuggling opium

5. A hairstyle, like a plait, that showed you supported the Qing emperors

Page 107 Quick Test: Mughal India

1. 150 million
2. It was said to be 1 million strong
3. Farm workers in India
4. Robert Fitch in 1583
5. Mostly silver, but sometimes with gold

Page 109 Quick Test: The West Indies: Fighting Back Against Slavery

1. To grow sugar
2. 1562/3
3. Escaped slaves in Jamaica who settled in the hills and resisted the British.
4. Ignatius Sancho
5. 1791

Pages 110–113 Review Questions

Page 110 The First World War

1. Gavrilo Princip [1]
2. 214 000 [1]
3. Enemy shelling [1]
4. The War Guilt Clause [1]
5. **One mark** for each valid observation (**5 marks** maximum). You might include the following observations:
   - Worries that people would starve.
   - Worries about widespread poverty.
   - Newspapers often show common opinion.
   - A drawback is that a cartoon might exaggerate.
   - It also mainly focuses on reparations, not other areas of the treaty.

For question 6 see Mark Scheme A.

6. Your answer might include mention of the following problems:
   - Unprepared for new technologies used by the enemy such as machine guns and mustard gas.
   - Rats; water causing disease/infections such as trench foot.

Page 111 The Second World War

1. January 1933 [1]
2. They did not want to risk the possibility of war and were more worried about the USSR [1]
3. Operation Sealion [1]
4. Over 6 million [1]

For question 5 see Mark Scheme A.

5. Your answer should give an opinion and at least three different reasons. Examples may include:
   - Hitler's order for the invasion of the Soviet Union in 1941.
   - The D-Day landings, which took place in 1944.
   - The German army was attacked in both the West and East.
   - Millions of soldiers were killed during the war in the East.

6. **One mark** for each valid observation (**5 marks** maximum). You might include the following observations:
   - Britain had to prevent the invasion in order to end the war.
   - British people were encouraged to do their duty to help the country.
   - Britain also relied on Commonwealth nations for support.
   - It shows the government understood how serious the Battle was.
   - A drawback is that it does not explain how Britain was to prepare for the invasion.

Page 112 The Creation of the Welfare State

1. Dirty water and cholera [1]
2. Germany [1]
3. 45 [1]
4. Doctors' throats [1]
5. **One mark** for each valid observation (**5 marks** maximum). You might include the following observations:
   - Doctors thought the government was interfering with their work.
   - They were opposed on political grounds.
   - Many doctors were conservative; Bevan was a Labour MP.
   - The source doesn't tell us about disagreements over pay.
   - It doesn't tell us how the issue was resolved.

For question 6 see Mark Scheme A.

6. Your answer might include the following reasons, with the best answers looking at a wide range of points:
   - Pensions not issued until 70 when life expectancy was 45 for most.
   - Labour Exchanges often provided only low-paid, part-time jobs.
   - Health care from National Insurance didn't extend to a worker's family.

Page 113 Britain's Place in the World 1945–Present

1. 1956 [1]
2. USA and USSR [1]
3. The Beatles and the Rolling Stones [1]
4. 82 per cent [1]

For questions 5 and 6 see Mark Scheme A.

5. Your answer should describe at least two different changes. Examples of changes since 1945 may include:
   - The number of women in work doubled from 6 million to 12 million.
   - The disappearance of traditional industries such as coal mining, shipbuilding and steel.
   - Huge growth in the use of technology.
   - The number of self-employed workers increased.

6. Your answer might include the following reasons, backed up with facts:
   - The introduction of the NHS and advanced medical care.
   - Increase in immigration from the Commonwealth following the Second World War.
   - Increase in life expectancy, with 16 per cent of the population over 65.

Page 114 Migration To and From the British Isles
1. 800 million [1]
2. The Caribbean [1]
3. Smallpox [1]
4. Their Catholic beliefs [1]

For questions 5 and 6 see Mark Scheme A.
5. Your answer should explain the impact of:
   * The shortage of workers.
   * Recruitment campaigns for companies such as London Transport and the NHS.
   * The impact of Acts such as the British Nationality Act.
6. Your answer might include the following problems:
   * The Notting Hill riots.
   * Cultural and language barriers.
   * Discrimination.

Page 114 The Kingdom of Benin
1. From European visitors and Benin's oral history [1]
2. On the walls of the Oba's Palace [1]
3. **See Mark Scheme A.** Your answer should explore at least two of the following reasons with arguments to support your answer:
   * to trade; to explore
   * to try to spread Christianity to the natives
   * to build an Empire
   * to civilize people they thought of as heathens and savages.

   Trade changed because other goods such as palm oil, pepper and ivory became less important and slaves, guns and brass manillas became more important.

Page 115 Qing China
1. Around 450 million [1]
2. The belief that the Emperor was appointed by God to rule – if he ruled well, he was left alone, if he ruled badly then he should be deposed and replaced. [1]
3. **See Mark Scheme A.** You should include at least three of the following causes of the war, backed up with explanations and facts to support your answer:
   * trade
   * wealth
   * the West's demand for colonies
   * China's policy of isolation
   * opium.

Page 115 Mughal India
1. 25 per cent [1]
2. In 1857, when it became part of the British India [1]
3. **See Mark Scheme A.** The most appropriate answer is probably to agree with the statement. You could refer to the following points to support your argument:
   * 15 per cent of the population were Muslims – but most of these were rulers and traders, who had conquered India and the Hindus.
   * As most people were relatively well off, at least in the beginning, it was easier to get on with everyone.
   * The Muslim rulers didn't force anyone to change their religion.

   * They employed Hindus, Buddhists, as well as Muslims.
   * Most rural Indians were Hindus and had little to do with Muslim authorities.
   * The Mughals kept the empire peaceful, at least until the 18th century.

   Your answer might contrast Mughal India with other, less tolerant, societies you have studied.

Page 115 The West Indies
1. 'Nanny of the Maroons' [1]
2. 5 million [1]
3. **See Mark Scheme A.** You should include at least three of the following reasons, backed up with explanations and facts to support your answer:
   * falling profits
   * revolts by slaves making the system unworkable
   * humanitarian ideas that slavery was wrong
   * the work of freed slaves in highlighting injustice
   * the French Revolution.

Page 116 Migration To and From the British Isles
1. 12th century [1]
2. Slaves [1]
3. The successful harvest of 1621 [1]
4. Taking their women [1]
5. **One mark** for each valid point (**5 marks** maximum). You might include the following points:
   * It is useful in telling us there was a lot of racism towards immigrants.
   * It doesn't tell us about poor housing conditions.
   * It doesn't tell us about race riots.
   * It doesn't tell us about young white men attacking immigrants over women.
   * It doesn't tell us about language/cultural barriers.

For question 6 see Mark Scheme A.
6. Your answer should include some of the following:
   * Jewish moneylenders recorded in the 12th century.
   * Romans bringing Africans to guard Hadrian's Wall.
   * Some seamen from the Empire settled in Britain after the First World War.

Page 117 The Kingdom of Benin/Qing China/Mughal India/The West Indies
1. In 1550 – to trade for pepper, ivory, palm oil and cloth [1]
2. In 1730 – other kingdoms were getting richer and overtaking Benin [1]
3. **See Mark Scheme A.** Your answer should include a range of the following views and outline your own conclusion supported with evidence and ideas:

   Should be returned: they were stolen, they belong in Benin (Nigeria), the people there should have access to their own history;

   Shouldn't be returned: they belong here, museums exist to explain history and culture, Benin can't look after them properly.
4. 32 per cent [1]

5. **a)** Jobs – 100 000 craftsmen made it; Income – rich people in the West really wanted it; Status – best in the world [4]

   b) Ended: West learnt how to do it for themselves; Copied China's techniques [2]

6. Akhbar [1]

7. Silks, textiles and spices [1]

8. **See Mark Scheme A.** There is no one correct answer to this, but most people would suggest that the terms of trade were very much in favour – eventually – of the West. Your answer should ideally discuss change over time, as well as interpretations. A good answer would explore the following:
   * Initially, the trade made India richer, bringing much silver to the country. In 1600, Mughal India was the biggest economy in the world. India had goods the West wanted – silk, pepper, etc.
   * As time went on, Britain especially became richer. The Industrial Revolution destroyed India's textile trade. Britain used Indian opium to trade with China for tea for Britain, and then learnt to grow tea in India. Britain's superior military might imposed control on the Mughals, for the benefit of Britain. India's farmers, instead of being richer than those in England, ended up much poorer.

9. Many of the native people had died or been killed and very few Europeans wanted to work there, but sugar needed a large labour force. [1]

10. Mary Prince [1]

11. **See Mark Scheme A.** There is no one correct answer to this. Your answer should explore the following contributing factors and outline your own conclusion supported with evidence and ideas:
    * The British Parliament
    * British public opinion, e.g. the sugar boycott
    * Freed black slaves like Equiano and Mary Prince
    * White abolitionists like Wilberforce and Clarkson.

Pages 118–125 Mixed Test-Style Questions

Page 118

1. **One mark** for each valid observation (**5 marks** maximum). You might include the following observations:
   * It shows soldiers fighting in battle.
   * One soldier has an arrow in his eye – could be Harold.
   * It shows what soldiers wore and the weapons they used.
   * It only shows one aspect of battle.
   * It was produced over 10 years after the event so it may not be very accurate.

2. **One mark** for each valid observation (**5 marks** maximum). You might include the following observations:
   * It is one person's view.
   * It is written over 10 years after the Black Death.
   * It doesn't mention the belief that bad air was a cause.
   * It doesn't mention the belief that the Black Death was a punishment from God.

Page 120

1. **One mark** for each correct answer (**5 marks** maximum).
   a) False **b)** True **c)** True **d)** False **e)** True

2. **One mark** for each valid observation (**5 marks** maximum). You might include the following observations:
   * It shows that Emmeline Pankhurst tried to justify her violent actions.
   * It shows that the Pankhursts wanted publicity for their cause, particularly from the newspapers.
   * It shows that Emmeline Pankhurst was an educated woman because she wrote a book.
   * It doesn't tell us about the effect or importance of non-violent protest organised by Millicent Fawcett.
   * It is only Emmeline Pankhurst's opinion. It does not look at events in detail.

Page 122

1. **One mark** for each valid observation (**5 marks** maximum). You might include the following observations:
   * It shows children under machines.
   * It shows inadequate clothing.
   * There is poor ventilation – there are very few windows.
   * There are no safety guards.
   * There are no supervisors.

2. **One mark** for each valid observation (**5 marks** maximum). You might include the following observations:
   * It is one person's view.
   * It is written only half way through the war.
   * It does not mention common views of life in the trenches.
   * The writer might have lied to reassure his family.
   * He seems very literate and possibly not working class so may not be representative.

Page 123

For marks for these questions see Mark Scheme A.

1. You need to use your imagination to answer this question, describing your motives and feelings with as much detail as possible. Your motives will depend on what kind of person you imagine yourself being:
   * If a king, going on a Crusade would bring you extra power and wealth and the support of the Pope.
   * If a lord, you would be going on a Crusade to gain wealth and land.
   * If a knight, you might be going on a Crusade because your king and lord demanded it. Also, as a knight you had a duty to protect the Christian Church.
   * Ordinary people went on Crusades to gain extra credit to get into heaven.
   * Criminals and thieves went on Crusades because it would mean their punishments would come to an end.
   * Priests and monks went on Crusades to participate in a holy war to regain the Holy Land.

2. Your answer should give a full explanation of the factors that forced King John to sign Magna Carta, and should

be supported with evidence. The main factors, in brief, were as follows:

- King John faced major financial problems.
- He also had major problems with the Church.
- King John had lost lots of English land in France.
- John had a quarrel with the barons, which he was losing.
- John was forced to sign to end this quarrel and to help end his other problems.

3. A good answer would cover the following points, and each point would be supported by a full explanation and evidence:

- The Reformation changed England from a Catholic country to a Protestant country.
- The King, rather than the Pope, was Head of the Church.
- Religious services were in English instead of Latin.
- The King gained wealth and power from the Church.
- The monasteries were dissolved.

Page 124

For marks for these questions see Mark Scheme A.

1. A good answer would cover the following points, supported by evidence:

- It was a conflict between two groups in the same country.
- It involved the trial and execution of a monarch.
- It was followed by a period without a monarchy.

2. A good answer would cover the following points, supported by evidence:

- From 1649, stability of government was required following the execution of the King. Cromwell retained the loyalty and support of the army.
- Cromwell had been a key figure in the execution of Charles and the destruction of the monarchy.
- The Lord Protector had many of the powers of a king, but was not answerable to Parliament.
- Cromwell feared many people would argue that he had helped execute the King for his own personal benefit.

3. A good answer would cover the following points, supported by evidence:

- Poverty among Irish farmers intensified by mass starvation following the disastrous potato harvest of 1845.

- Millions faced a difficult and cramped journey to the USA, often only affordable for one family member.
- On arrival in New York, immigrants had to undergo stringent medical checks at Ellis Island.
- Those able to stay faced life in a squalid tenement block and being stigmatised for their Catholic beliefs.

Page 125

For marks for these questions see Mark Scheme A.

1. A good answer would cover the following points, supported by evidence:

- Support due to a number of political, economic and social motivations.
- The manifesto of the emerging Labour Party focused heavily on welfare reform. A growing trade union movement was also pressing for better working conditions.
- Recruitment of soldiers for the Boer War had shown most working-class men to be unfit for service.
- Lloyd George had genuine compassion for the working class.

2. A good answer would cover the following points, supported by evidence:

- The Soviet army appeared to be very weak and could easily be defeated in 1941.
- Three million soldiers were sent to fight and the Germans planned to use the tactic of Blitzkrieg warfare.
- Early German successes meant that it looked like Moscow and Leningrad could be easily captured, but in practice they never were.
- The Battle of Stalingrad was brutal, and the harsh conditions meant that many soldiers starved or froze to death.

3. A good answer would cover the following points, supported by evidence:

- The development of popular culture – including music, film and fashion.
- The impact of the legalisation of abortion and the introduction of the contraceptive pill.
- Increasing ownership of consumer goods.
- The rise of the teenager, youth consumerism and the changing roles of women.

Timeline

1066 Battle of Hastings; William is crowned king.

1066–76 Rebellion of Hereward the Wake.

1069 Rebellion against William in northern England.

1085–86 Domesday Book compiled.

1087 William I dies.

1096–99 The First Crusade.

c1120 Origins of the Benin Empire.

1147–49 The Second Crusade.

1170 Archbishop Thomas A'Becket murdered in Canterbury.

1170 Eweka becomes Oba of Benin.

1187 Battle of Hattin.

1189–92 The Third Crusade.

1199 John becomes King.

1202–04 The Fourth Crusade.

1204 King John loses Normandy to France.

1205 King John has a major argument with the Pope.

1209 The Pope excommunicates John.

1212 The Children's Crusade.

1214 War breaks out between John and the barons.

1215 John signs Magna Carta.

1265 England's first parliament meets.

June 1348 Black Death arrives in England at Melcombe Regis (Weymouth) in Dorset.

Aug 1348 Black Death hits Bristol.

Sept 1348 Black Death reaches London.

Jan 1349 Parliament stops meeting due to the plague.

Jan–Feb 1349 Plague reaches East Anglia and the Midlands.

April 1349 Black Death reported in Wales.

July 1349 Black Death hits Ireland.

1377 Richard II becomes King at the age of 10.

1380 Poll Tax is introduced.

May–June 1381 Peasants' Revolt breaks out in Essex and Kent.

1381 Poll Tax is withdrawn.

1440 Ewuare the Great makes Benin stronger than ever.

1472 First Europeans – the Portuguese – arrive in Benin.

1492 Columbus arrives in the Caribbean on his first voyage.

1500–1600 Europeans develop colonies in the Americas.

1500 The feudal system ends; all Englishmen are freemen.

1509 Henry VIII becomes King.

1526 First Mughal emperor.

1530 Benin stops selling slaves to Europeans.

1533 Henry divorces Catherine of Aragon.

1534 Henry VIII makes himself Supreme Head of the Church in England.

1536 Henry begins closing monasteries.

1547 Edward VI makes England a Protestant country.

1550 First English traders arrive in Benin.

1553 Mary I becomes Queen; Counter-Reformation begins.

1556 Akbar becomes Mughal emperor.

1558 Mary I dies; replaced by the Protestant Elizabeth I.

1562–63 First British triangular slave trade voyage.

1608 First English ship arrives in Mughal India.

1619 First group of slaves arrive in North America.

1620 Pilgrim Fathers arrive in America.

1628 Shah Jehan becomes Mughal emperor.

August 1642 English Civil War breaks out.

October 1642 Battle of Edgehill.

1644 First Qing emperor rules the whole of China.

July 1644 Battle of Marston Moor.

June 1645 Battle of Naseby.

January 1647 Charles is given to Parliament.

November 1647 Charles escapes.

August 1648 Charles is recaptured.

January 1649 Charles is executed; the monarchy is abolished and England becomes a republic.

1653 Cromwell and his army march to Parliament and close it down. Cromwell is elected as Lord Protector.

1655 Cromwell divides the country into districts and puts army Major-Generals in charge.

1655–57 Rule of the Major-Generals established to stop opposition towards Cromwell and protect law and order.

1657 Cromwell is offered the crown, but refuses. He is given extra powers as Lord Protector.

1658 Cromwell dies of ill health.

1658 Cromwell's son Richard becomes Lord Protector.

1659 Richard resigns due to lack of support.

1660 Charles II returns from Holland and restores the monarchy.

1700s Northern US states abolish slavery but it remains important in the South.

1730 Benin restarts the slave trade.

1735 Qianlong becomes Qing emperor.

1740 British sign peace treaty with the Jamaican Maroons, having been unable to defeat them in battle.

1769 Richard Arkwright invents water frame.

1769 James Watt improves steam engine.

1772 The Somerset Case confirms that it is illegal to have slaves in Britain.

1773 Scots arrive in Canada.

1774 Ignatius Sancho becomes the first black person to vote.

1789 French Revolution begins.

1791 Revolt in Haiti, led by Toussaint L'Ouverture.

1804 Haiti becomes the first Caribbean nation to gain its independence.

1807 The Slave Trade Abolition Act in Britain.

1820s Only men aged over 21 with property can vote.

1830 First passenger railway opens.

1831 Mary Prince's autobiography is published – the first by a female former slave.

1832 Reform Act.

1833 The Slavery Abolition Act in Britain.

1836 London artisans form the London Working Men's Association.

1839 Chartist petition.

1839 Newport Uprising.

1840 First opium war between Britain and China.

1840s Many Irish leave for America.

1848 Public Health Act.

1848 End of Chartism.

1853 Smallpox vaccination compulsory.

1854 Improvements in hospital hygiene.

1857 End of Mughals – India becomes part of British empire following the Indian Mutiny.

1861–65 American Civil War.

1864 Factory Act improves standards and safety measures.

1865 Slavery is abolished in the Americas.

1867 Parliamentary Reform Act increases the number of men who can vote.

1870 and 1882 Laws passed to allow women to keep income and property after marriage.

1872 National Society for Women's Suffrage formed.

1872 Ballot Act attempts to end bribery and corruption.

1874 Factory Act reduces working hours.

1875 Public Health Act provides clean water in towns.

1884 Parliamentary Reform Act.

1894 Manchester ship canal opens.

1897 Millicent Fawcett forms the National Union of Women's Suffrage Societies.

1897 As part of the 'Scramble for Africa', a British army arrives in Benin, destroys the city, and makes Benin part of the British Empire.

1903 Women's Social and Political Union formed by the Pankhursts.

1905 Two Suffragettes arrested in Manchester.

1906 Suffragette protest at Downing Street.

1906 Free school meals.

1907 School Medical Inspectors Act.

1908 Children's Charter and old age pensions.

1908 Suffragette protest rally in Hyde Park.

1909 Labour Exchanges set up.

1911 A revolution results in the end of the Qing Empire.

1911 National Insurance Act.

1911 220 suffragettes arrested for a series of violent protests.

1913 Emily Davison killed by a horse at the Epsom Derby.

June 1914 Franz Ferdinand assassinated.

28 July 1914 War breaks out.

February 1915 Gallipoli campaign begins.

December 1915 Gallipoli campaign ends in disaster.

1916 Lloyd George becomes Prime Minister.

Feb–July 1916 The Battle of Verdun.

July–Nov 1916 The Battle of the Somme.

11 November 1918 The First World War ends.

1918 Women over 30 who own property given the vote.

28 June 1919 The Treaty of Versailles signed.

1928 All women given the right to vote in Britain.

1933 Hitler becomes Chancellor and subsequently Führer.

1936 German troops march into the Rhineland.

1938 Austria and Germany unite.

1938 Appeasement agreement (Munich Pact).

1939 Hitler invades Czechoslovakia and Poland.

3 Sept 1939 Britain and France declare war on Germany.

1940 Evacuation of Dunkirk.

1940 The Battle of Britain.

1941 Germany invades the Soviet Union.

1942 Soviet Union starts to push the German army back.

1943 German army surrenders at Stalingrad.

1944 D-Day landings take place.

1944 Education Act (implemented 1945); school leaving age raised to 15.

30 April 1945 Germany surrenders; end of Second World War.

1945 Labour responsible for post-war consensus.

1945 Family allowances introduced.

1946 National Insurance Act extended.

1948 National Assistance Act to help those not covered by National Insurance.

1948 British Nationality Act.

1948 National Health Service introduced.

1949 Britain joins NATO.

1955 Commercial television begins.

1962 Commonwealth Immigration Act in Britain.

1964 Civil Rights Act passed in USA.

1965 and 1968 Race Relations Act in Britain.

1968 Commonwealth Immigrants Act in Britain.

1971 Immigration Act in Britain.

1972 Miners go on strike.

1973 Britain joins the European Community.

1979 The Winter of Discontent leads to Labour losing the general election. Margaret Thatcher becomes Britain's first female prime minister.

1991 The Internet becomes available to the public.

1997 Labour, led by Tony Blair, wins the general election.

2010 Labour loses power to a Conservative–Liberal Democrat coalition.

2020 Britain leaves the EU.

Index

Collins

KS3
History

Workbook

Philippa Birch, Steve McDonald,
Rachelle Pennock and Alf Wilkinson

Contents

Rethink Revision

Have you ever taken part in a quiz and thought '*I know this*!', but no matter how hard you scrabbled around in your brain you just couldn't come up with the answer?

It's very frustrating when this happens, but in a fun situation it doesn't really matter. However, in tests and assessments, it is essential that you can recall the relevant information when you need to.

Most students think that revision is about making sure you **know** *stuff*, but it is also about being confident that you can **retain** that *stuff* over time and **recall** it when needed.

Revision that Really Works

Experts have discovered that there are two techniques that help you to retain and recall information and consistently produce better results in tests and exams compared to other revision techniques.

Applying these techniques to your KS3 revision will ensure you get better results in tests and assessments and will have all the relevant knowledge at your fingertips when you start studying for your GCSEs.

It really isn't rocket science either – you simply need to:

* **test yourself** on each topic as many times as possible
* **leave a gap** between the test sessions.

It is most effective if you leave a good period of time between the test sessions, e.g. between a week and a month. The idea is that just as you start to forget the information, you force yourself to recall it again, keeping it fresh in your mind.

Three Essential Revision Tips

1 Use Your Time Wisely
* Allow yourself plenty of time
* Try to start revising six months before tests and assessments – it's more effective and less stressful
* Your revision time is precious so use it wisely – using the techniques described on this page will ensure you revise effectively and efficiently and get the best results
* Don't waste time re-reading the same information over and over again – it's time-consuming and not effective!

2 Make a Plan
* Identify all the topics you need to revise
* Plan at least five sessions for each topic
* A one-hour session should be ample to test yourself on the key ideas for a topic
* Spread out the practice sessions for each topic – the optimum time to leave between each session is about one month but, if this isn't possible, just make the gaps as big as realistically possible.

3 Test Yourself
* Methods for testing yourself include: quizzes, practice questions, flashcards, past-papers, explaining a topic to someone else.
* Don't worry if you get an answer wrong – provided you check what the correct answer is, you are more likely to get the same or similar questions right in future!

Visit **collins.co.uk/collinsks3revision** for more information about the benefits of these revision techniques and for further guidance on how to plan ahead and make them work for you.

Britain 1066–1509

The Norman Conquest

1 Three people claimed the throne of England in 1066 after the death of King Edward the Confessor: Harald Hardrada, Harold Godwinson and William of Normandy.

a) What was Hardrada's claim?

_____

_____ **[2]**

b) What was William's claim?

_____

_____ **[2]**

c) What was Harold's claim?

_____

_____ **[2]**

d) Who had the strongest claim?

_____

_____ **[2]**

e) Why did William win the Battle of Hastings?

_____

_____

_____ **[3]**

2 Study Source A and answer the questions that follow.

Source A: An extract from the Domesday Book for Elstow, in Bedfordshire

> **ELSTOW [ELNESTOV]** answers for 3½ hides. The nuns of St Mary's hold it from Countess Judith. Land for seven ploughs. In lordship 2 ploughs. 14 villagers have 5 ploughs. 11 smallholders and 4 slaves. 1 mill at 24s; meadow for 4 ploughs; woodland, 60 pigs. Value 100s; when acquired 40s; before 1066 £10. 4 Freeman held this manor. They were King Edward's men.

a) Who owned Elstow? _____ [1]

b) How much land was there in Elstow? _____ [1]

c) How many people lived there?

_____ [1]

d) How much was Elstow worth in 1066 and in 1086?

_____

_____ [2]

e) What is the significance of the (water) mill?

_____

_____ [2]

f) Why did William order his officials to make the Domesday Book?

_____

_____

_____ [3]

g) Why is the Domesday Book such an important piece of evidence about life in the Norman period? In your answer, try to cover the survey's strengths and weaknesses as a historical piece of evidence.

_____

_____

_____

_____

_____

_____ [5]

Total Marks _____ / 26

Christendom and the Crusades

1 Study Source A and then answer the questions below.

Source A: A simplified plan of a medieval monastery

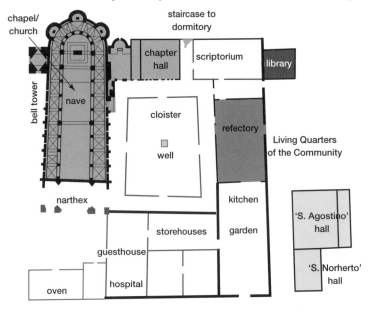

a) Which is the most important building? How can you tell?

....

.... **[2]**

b) Apart from praying, what else does the plan indicate that monks did?

....

.... **[3]**

c) Who were 'the community'?

....

.... **[2]**

d) Why were monasteries so rich in medieval times?

....

.... **[2]**

e) Why did men choose to become monks? Give two reasons.

....

.... **[2]**

2 Study Sources B and C and then answer the questions that follow.

Source B: A modern historian on the struggle between Henry II and Thomas Becket

The attack was the conclusion of a long struggle between king and archbishop. Great issues were at stake. Henry II was a remarkable and intelligent ruler, who had a vision of a land in which justice should be available to all, and all should be equal under royal law. Thomas had his own vision, believing that the authority of the Church should be supreme in all things, and that the King should rule as the Church's representative in the secular world. Royal interference in the Church's affairs should be ended.

Source C: A Victorian image of the death of Thomas Becket

a) Study Source B. What were Henry and Thomas arguing about?

....

....

.... [3]

b) How useful is Source C in helping us to understand the quarrel?

....

....

....

.... [3]

c) Which source do you think is more useful in understanding what happened to Thomas Becket? Why?

....

....

.... [2]

Total Marks .... / 19

Magna Carta

1 Study Source A and answer the questions that follow.

Source A: from Henrietta Marshall, *Our Island Story*, published 1905

> No king of England has ever been so bad as John. He was a bad son, a bad brother, a bad king and a bad man.

a) Why might the author describe John as a bad son?

_____ [1]

b) Why might the author describe John as a bad brother?

_____

_____ [2]

c) Why might the author describe John as a bad man?

_____

_____ [2]

d) In your opinion, was John a bad king?

_____

_____

_____

_____ [4]

2 In 1265, Henry III and Simon de Montfort called a Parliament.

a) Why was Parliament called?

....

.... [2]

b) How was this Parliament different to any that had been called before?

....

.... [1]

c) Who was this Parliament made up of and how were members chosen?

....

....

....

.... [4]

d) How is the organisation and power of the 1265 Parliament similar to and different from Parliament today?

....

....

....

.... [3]

Total Marks .... / 19

Britain 1066–1509

The Black Death

1 No one at the time knew what caused the Black Death. So how were people treated who caught the plague?

a) What measures were taken by individuals to try and prevent the spread of the disease and to treat patients?

[3]

b) Were these treatments effective?

[1]

c) How did authorities try to make the towns safer places to live?

[3]

d) What part did the Church play in treating the disease?

[3]

2 The impact of the Black Death was very severe. Over 33 per cent of the population – perhaps 1.5 million people – died in England. Below is a list of the social and economic effects of the Black Death.

- [ ] Many houses collapsed or fell into disrepair.

- [ ] Wages went up.

- [ ] Prices went up, especially of foodstuffs.

- [ ] A law was passed to make sure wages stayed the same.

- [ ] Rich people found they could not employ as many servants.

- [ ] There was a shortage of priests as many had died.

- [ ] Lots of villages were deserted and fell into ruin.

- [ ] People went to church less.

- [ ] People moved around the country more, looking for better jobs.

- [ ] It was easier for a lower-class person to improve their wealth, income and status.

a) Number the boxes to rank these 10 effects of the Black Death in order of importance, with (1) being most important and (10) being least important. You might think some are of equal importance so you can group effects if you wish. **[1]**

b) Explain why you have chosen your most important effect.

_____

_____

_____ **[3]**

c) Explain why you have chosen your least important effect.

_____

_____

_____ **[3]**

d) When did the Black Death die out?

_____ **[1]**

Total Marks _____ / 18

Britain 1066–1509

The Peasants' Revolt

1 The Peasants' Revolt started in May 1381 in Essex and Kent. Thousands of people marched on London demanding to see the King and wanting him to intervene to make their lives better. The table below shows some of the causes of the revolt, according to historians.

	Long	Medium	Short
The Poll Taxes of 1377, 1379 and 1380			
Resentment of peasants at having to work two or three days a week for their lords			
The preaching of John Ball			
Richard II was a new, young and inexperienced king			
The Black Death			
The Statute of Labourers 1351			
England doing badly in the Hundred Years War and increasing French attacks in the South and East			
The attempt to collect unpaid Poll Tax in Fobbing, Essex, on 30 May 1381			
The feudal system			

a) Place a tick in the appropriate column to indicate whether each cause was a long-term, medium-term or short-term cause of the Revolt. **[9]**

b) Which of these causes do you think was most important? Why?

....

.... **[2]**

c) Which of these causes do you think was least important? Why?

....

.... **[2]**

d) When, in your opinion, did the Peasants' Revolt become inevitable?

....

.... **[2]**

2 Below is a list of the key events surrounding the Peasants' Revolt.

a) Number the boxes to indicate the chronological order of the events.

☐ Peasants go home

☐ Black Death

☐ Richard II speaks to the peasants at Mile End

☐ Attempt to collect Poll Tax in Fobbing

☐ Richard II sets the army on any rebels

☐ Richard II tries to speak to the peasants

☐ Richard II promises the peasants he will meet all their demands

☐ Poll Tax introduced

☐ Many rebels killed

☐ Peasants march on London

☐ Statute of Labourers

☐ Wat Tyler meets the King and is killed by the Mayor of London   [12]

b) Who was the most significant individual in the Peasants' Revolt – Wat Tyler, John Ball or Richard II?

....

....

....

[3]

Total Marks .... / 30

Britain 1509–1745

Reformation and Counter-Reformation

1 How did Henry VIII change the Church?

....

.... **[2]**

2 How did Edward VI change the Church?

....

.... **[2]**

3 How did Mary I change the Church?

....

.... **[2]**

4 In your opinion, which of these three monarchs changed the Church the most?

....

....

....

.... **[4]**

5 Why were there so many changes in the Church in Tudor times?

....

....

....

.... **[4]**

6 Study Sources A and B and then answer the questions that follow.

Source A: The inside of a Catholic church

Source B: The inside of a Protestant church

a) What differences are there between the Catholic church in Source A and the Protestant church in Source B? Give two examples.

_____

_____ [2]

b) What similarities are there between the Catholic church in Source A and the Protestant church in Source B? Give three examples.

_____

_____ [3]

c) Using the sources and your own knowledge, what consequence would there be for religion in England from a growing number of Protestant churches? Explain your answer.

_____

_____ [2]

Total Marks _____ / 21

Britain 1509–1745

The English Civil Wars

1 When did the Civil Wars start?

.... [1]

2 When did the Civil Wars end?

.... [1]

3 What part did King Charles I play in causing the Civil Wars?

....

....

.... [3]

4 What part did Parliament play in causing the Civil Wars?

....

....

.... [3]

5 In your opinion, who was most to blame – Parliament or King?

....

.... [2]

6 Study Sources A, B and C and then answer the questions that follow.

Source A: **Source B:**   **Source C:**

a) What type of soldier is shown in Source A? What weapon did he use? What role did he play in Civil War battles?

....

.... **[3]**

b) What type of soldier is shown in Source B? What weapon did he use? What role did he play in Civil War battles?

....

.... **[3]**

c) What type of soldier is shown in Source C? What weapon did he use? What role did he play in Civil War battles?

....

.... **[3]**

d) What was new about the New Model Army?

....

....

.... **[3]**

Total Marks .... / 22

The Interregnum

1 How did Cromwell change life in England?

[4]

2 Did people like his changes? Explain your answer.

[2]

3 In 1653, Parliament made Cromwell Lord Protector of England. Give two ways this was similar to and two ways this was different from being King of England.

[4]

4 In 1660, Charles, the son of the executed King Charles I, was invited back to London and crowned as King Charles II.

Study Source A and answer the questions that follow.

Source A: A Modern historian talks about Charles II

> Known as the 'Merry Monarch', Charles II's reign was an era of flamboyant fashions and courtly excess. He wanted a good time. People felt it a relief to return to normal life after 10 years of Puritan rule. Charles is thought to have had 12 illegitimate children and many mistresses. He loved balls and the theatre. He showed that it was now alright to have fun.

a) What was Charles II's nickname?

.... [1]

b) Why was Charles II known by this nickname?

....

.... [2]

5 Why was Charles II made King?

....

....

.... [3]

6 What changes did Charles II make after becoming King of England?

....

....

.... [3]

Total Marks .... / 19

Transatlantic Slave Trade/Abolition of the Slave Trade

1 Why were so many Africans taken to the Americas?

.... **[1]**

2 Why did many Europeans think it was acceptable to use Africans as slaves?

.... **[1]**

3 Describe what life was like for slaves on a plantation in the Americas.

....

....

....

.... **[3]**

4 Which groups of people campaigned for the abolition of the slave trade in Britain?

....

....

....

.... **[3]**

5 Who opposed abolition?

....

.... **[2]**

6 When did the legal use of slaves end in the British Empire?

.... **[1]**

7 When was slavery abolished in the USA?

.... **[1]**

8 When did the UN attempt to end slavery everywhere? Was this successful?

_____

_____ **[2]**

9 Study Source A, then answer the following questions:

Source A: A modern historian's view

> After the abolition of slavery, most available work was on the very same plantations that former enslaved people had worked on; the wages paid by employers were low, and ex-slaves had inadequate rights to land. Rent and taxes were high, and many slaves could not get jobs. Many went to live on the poorest land, away from the plantations and tried to grow their own food. They found it difficult to make ends meet, let alone make their lives better now they were free. Meanwhile slave owners were paid large sums in compensation by the British Government for having their property (their slaves) taken away from them.

a) How did abolition affect owners?

_____

_____

_____ **[3]**

b) How did abolition affect slaves in the Caribbean?

_____

_____

_____ **[3]**

c) How useful is this source in helping us to understand the impact of abolition on slaves?

_____

_____ **[2]**

Total Marks _____ / 22

Britain as the First Industrial Nation

1 Who was known as the 'Father of the Industrial Revolution'?

[1]

2 How were the machines in the early factories powered? [1]

3 Study Source A and answer the questions that follow.

Source A: Adapted from an obituary of Sir Richard Arkwright in the *Annual Register* 1792

Sir Richard Arkwright died this year on the 3rd August 1792, at his home in Cromford, in Derbyshire, aged 59. He leaves one son and one daughter. He was buried at Matlock on the 9th August. His remains will be removed to Cromford as soon as the Church, begun by him, is completed. Sir Richard began his life as a humble barber in a village near Manchester. When he died he was a very rich man. His personal property and wealth has been estimated at nearly half a million pounds. His rise to wealth began almost by accident – he bought a machine called a Spinning Jenny. (Its inventor, in need of funds, sold it for £50!) By genius and hard work he then set about developing and perfecting a system of machinery for spinning, which he introduced to his new factory at Cromford, in Derbyshire. This gave permanent employment to many thousands. By all this good work Sir Richard has made the country richer. Sir Richard, we are told, not only knew how to make money, he could also keep it. He was so careful how he spent his money, that some would say he was mean. Even if he was not a great man, he was certainly a very useful person.

a) Do you think the writer of Source A knew Arkwright? Are there any clues in the passage that help you decide?

[2]

b) Do you think the writer liked Arkwright? Choose some words or phrases from the passage to use in your answer.

[2]

c) Which of the following does the obituary suggest that Arkwright was? **i)** An inventor; **ii)** A good employer; **iii)** A successful entrepreneur; **iv)** Lucky. Explain your answer.

[4]

4 Study Sources B and C and then answer the questions that follow.

Source B: A modern historian's view

> Sir Richard Arkwright was a business genius of the first order. The founder of the modern factory system, he was the creator of a new industrial society that transformed England into the workshop of the world. He built houses for his workers, a school and a church.

Source C: An interview with John Reed who worked in Arkwright's Cromford factory in 1842

> I went to work at the cotton factory of Messrs Arkwright at the age of nine. I was then a fine strong, healthy lad, and straight in every limb. I earned 2s. per week at first, for seventy-two hours' work. I continued to work in this factory for ten years, getting gradually higher wages, till I had 6s. 3d. per week; which is the highest wages I ever had. I gradually became a cripple, till at the age of nineteen I was unable to stand at the machine, and I was forced to give it up. I have been made a miserable cripple, as you see, and cast off by those who had benefited from my labour, without a single penny.

a) What does the modern historian say about Arkwright? Do you think he likes him? How can you tell?

[3]

b) What does John Reed say about Arkwright? Do you think he liked him? How can you tell?

[3]

c) Why do these sources give such different views about Arkwright and the Industrial Revolution?

[5]

Total Marks / 21

Democratic Reform

1 What were the key changes made by the 1832 Reform Act?

....

....

....   **[3]**

2 Study Source A and then answer the questions that follow.

Source A: The six points of the People's Charter that set out the Chartists' main demands, May 1838

The Six Points
OF THE
PEOPLE'S
CHARTER.

1. A VOTE for every man twenty-one years of age, of sound mind, and not undergoing punishment for crime.

2. THE BALLOT.—To protect the elector in the exercise of his vote.

3. NO PROPERTY QUALIFICATION for Members of Parliament —thus enabling the constituencies to return the man of their choice, be he rich or poor.

4. PAYMENT OF MEMBERS, thus enabling an honest trades-man, working man, or other person, to serve a constituency, when taken from his business to attend to the interests of the country.

5. EQUAL CONSTITUENCIES, securing the same amount of representation for the same number of electors, instead of allowing small constituencies to swamp the votes of large ones.

6. ANNUAL PARLIAMENTS, thus presenting the most effectual check to bribery and intimidation, since though a constituency might be bought once in seven years (even with the ballot), no purse could buy a constituency (under a system of universal suffrage) in each ensuing twelvemonth; and since members, when elected for a year only, would not be able to defy and betray their constituents as now.

a) If you were a worker in 1838, which of these six points would you think most important?

....

....   **[2]**

b) Which would you think was least important?

....

....   **[2]**

c) Why do you think Parliament and the Government ignored the petition?

....

....

.... **[3]**

3 What were the key changes made by the 1867 Reform Act?

....

....

.... **[3]**

4 What were the key changes made by the 1872 Reform Act?

....

....

.... **[3]**

5 What were the key changes made by the 1884 Reform Act?

....

....

.... **[3]**

6 Which of these Acts, in your opinion, was the most important? Why?

....

....

....

.... **[4]**

7 Was Britain a democratic country by 1884?

....

.... **[2]**

Total Marks .... / 25

Britain 1901–Present

Women's Suffrage

1 Which of the following could women **not do** in 1860? Tick all that apply. [3]

Keep their own property when they married ☐

Keep their own income when they married ☐

Vote in a general election ☐

Become a guardian of the Poor Law/Workhouse ☐

2 Which of the following could women **not do** after 1882? [1]

Keep their own property when they married ☐

Keep their own income when they married ☐

Vote in a general election ☐

Become a guardian of the Poor Law/Workhouse ☐

3 Which of the following could women **not do** in 1900? [1]

Keep their own property when they married ☐

Keep their own income when they married ☐

Vote in a general election ☐

Become a guardian of the Poor Law/Workhouse ☐

4 Why was it thought women should have so few rights?

....

.... [3]

5 When was the first attempt to change the law to allow women to vote?

.... [1]

6 a) When was the National Society for Women's Suffrage set up? .... [1]

b) How successful was it? Explain your answer.

....

.... [2]

7 **a)** Which group was set up by Millicent Fawcett in 1897?

.... [1]

b) What were their aims? How did they try to achieve them?

....

....

....

....

....

.... [5]

c) How successful were they? Explain your answer.

....

.... [2]

8 Read Source A and study pages 62–65 of the revision guide section of this book. Then answer the questions that follow.

Source A: A modern historian's view

> In 1903, a new organisation, the Women's Social and Political Union (WSPU), was set up by Emmeline Pankhurst and her daughters. They wanted the vote and they wanted it now. They had little time for the NUWSS and its peaceful ways. They wanted to make sure Parliament gave women the vote and they were prepared to do anything necessary to achieve this.

a) In what ways was the WSPU similar to the NUWSS and how was it different?   [5]

Similar to NUWSS	Different to NUWSS

b) Which organisation, in your opinion, was more successful (if any)? Why?

....

....

.... [3]

Total Marks .... / 28

Britain 1901–Present

The First World War

1 When and where was Archduke Franz Ferdinand assassinated?

[2]

2 What date (day, month and year) was the armistice which ended the First World War?

[1]

3 Why were so many soldiers killed in the fighting on the Western Front?

[2]

4 Study Source A and then answer the question that follows.

Source A: A modern historian describes fighting on the Western Front in 1918

Smoke was used to obscure the battlefield and protect the infantry who were equipped with light machine guns and rifle grenades. They were expected to move fast. If they came upon a German strongpoint they were ordered to go round it, not attack it head on. Next, came the heavy machine guns. Behind these, the mortars. Then the tanks, used to destroy any remaining barbed wire or other obstacles. Flying above were aircraft, guiding the infantry and tanks, letting the artillery know where the targets were and shooting or bombing the Germans themselves whenever possible. The artillery provided a creeping barrage, moving slowly forward, just ahead of the infantry, and preventing the Germans from shooting at the advancing troops. They also delivered poisonous gas shells. Next came supply tanks, bringing up ammunition and reinforcements in order to keep the attack moving. All was carefully coordinated. It was a war of movement. And it worked! Over 400000 prisoners were taken, and 7000 heavy guns captured in a few days. The front line around Ypres moved forward 13 kilometres in a single day.

What new tactics were used by the Allies in 1918?

[2]

5 **a)** Look at the list of countries fighting in 1914. Tick the appropriate box to indicate whether each country gained or lost territory during the First World War.   **[5]**

Country	Gained	Lost
Britain		
France		
Germany		
Austria-Hungary		
Turkey (Ottoman Empire)		

b) What do you notice about your list?

....

....   **[2]**

6 Study Source B and then answer the questions that follow.

Source B: Maps of Europe in 1914 and 1919

Map of Europe 1914   Map of Europe 1919

a) What big change do you notice?

....

....   **[2]**

b) Do you think these new countries made Europe safer after the war or more dangerous?

....

....

....

....   **[3]**

Total Marks .... / 19

Britain 1901–Present

The Second World War

1 When did Hitler come to power in Germany? What were his aims?

[3]

2 When did Chamberlain become Prime Minister of Britain? What were his policies in relation to Hitler?

[3]

3 When did Roosevelt become President of the USA? What was his approach to Europe?

[2]

4 When did the Communists come to power in Russia? What did the West think the Communists wanted?

[2]

5 In your opinion, which of the above was the most important cause of the Second World War? Why?

[3]

6 What was the Bomber Theory?

_____

_____ **[2]**

7 Study Sources A and B and then answer the questions that follow.

Source A: London 1940

Source B: Berlin 1945

a) What has happened? Does this prove the Bomber Theory?

_____

_____

_____ **[3]**

b) How useful to historians are these photographs as evidence of the fighting in the Second World War?

_____

_____

_____

_____

_____ **[4]**

Total Marks _____ / 22

Britain 1901–Present

The Creation of the Welfare State

1. Use the information in the following table to complete the timeline below. **[8]**

Beveridge Report published	Prescription charge introduced
NHS set up	Free School meals introduced
Old Age pensions introduced	National Insurance Act
Labour Exchanges set up	School Medical Inspectors introduced

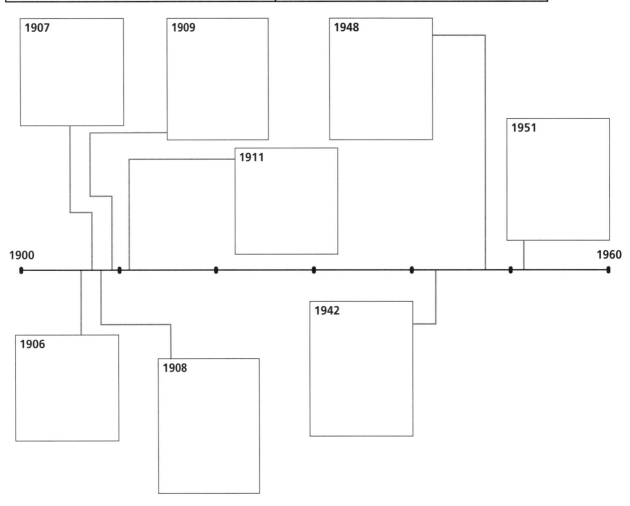

2. Why were many doctors opposed to the creation of the NHS?

.... **[1]**

3. How did the introduction of the NHS affect patients?

....

....

.... **[3]**

4) In his 1942 report, William Beveridge identified the 'Five Giants of Evil' that Britain needed to overcome if it was to recover from the war. What were they?

[5]

5) Study Source A and then answer the questions that follow.

Source A: A poster issued by Church Action on Poverty in 2013

BRITAIN ISN'T EATING.

FOOD BANK

Church Action
on Poverty

**THOUSANDS ARE GOING HUNGRY BECAUSE OF BENEFIT CHANGES.
CALL FOR URGENT ACTION: WWW.CHURCH-POVERTY.ORG.UK/WTB**

a) What is the message of the poster?

[2]

b) What is the purpose of the poster?

[1]

c) How useful is the poster in telling us about how successful the Welfare State had been in 2013 at reducing inequality in society?

[4]

Total Marks .... / 24

Britain 1901–Present

Britain's Place in the World 1945–Present

1. Name two major changes during the 1950s.

   [2]

2. Name two major changes during the 1960s.

   [2]

3. Name two major changes during the 1970s.

   [2]

4. Name two major changes during the 1980s.

   [2]

5. Name two major changes during the 1990s.

   [2]

6. Which decade, in your opinion, saw the greatest changes of all?

   [4]

7. When was Margaret Thatcher, Britain's first female Prime Minister, elected?

   [1]

8 Study Source A and answer the questions that follow:

Source A: Did Margaret Thatcher transform Britain's economy for better or worse? (Larry Elliott, *The Guardian*, 8 April 2013)

Reversing Britain's long-term economic decline … The last remnants of the postwar consensus were swept away in the ensuing decade – a period that saw the crushing of the trade unions, the Big Bang in the City, council house sales, the privatisation of large chunks of industry, the encouragement of inward investment, tax cuts, attempts to roll back the state, a deep manufacturing recession, a boom in North Sea oil production, and support for the creation of a single market in Europe.

As far as her supporters are concerned, this radical transformation worked. Britain ceased to be the sick man of Europe and entered the 1990s with its reputation enhanced. The economy had become more productive, more competitive and more profitable. Deep-seated and long overdue reforms of the 1980s paved the way for the long 16-year boom between 1992 and 2008.

To her detractors, Thatcher is the prime minister who wiped out more than 15% of Britain's industrial base with her dogmatic monetarism, squandered the once-in-a-lifetime windfall of North Sea oil on unemployment pay and tax cuts, and made the UK the unbalanced, unequal country it is today …

a) According to Larry Elliott, what were Mrs Thatcher's greatest achievements?

[3]

b) According to Larry Elliott, what were Mrs Thatcher's greatest failings?

[3]

c) Why do you think Mrs Thatcher divides opinion in Britain so much?

[2]

9 One historian stated that Thatcher's greatest achievement was the fact that she became Prime Minister at all. Do you agree?

[4]

Total Marks _____ / 27

British Social History

Migration To and From the British Isles

1 Historians tend to split reasons for migration into two – 'push' factors that force people to leave their home and 'pull' factors that attract them to a new country. Sort the following reasons into 'push factors' and 'pull factors'.

better education opportunities; war; unemployment; better standard of living; plenty of jobs available; poverty; better housing; lack of opportunity

Push factor	Pull factor

[8]

2 Number the following list of immigrants to show the order in which they came to Britain.

☐ Jewish migrants from Russia and Poland

☐ Irish

☐ Soldiers in the Roman army

☐ Caribbean migrants

☐ Vikings

☐ Normans

☐ Anglo-Saxons

☐ Huguenots

☐ citizens of the EU

☐ Commonwealth citizens from Asia   [10]

3 What has been the impact of migration on Britain since 1945?

....

....

....

....

....

....

[5]

4 Look at the following sources and then answer the questions below.

Source A: A 19th-century poster

Source B: A poster from the 1950s

a) Where are both posters trying to persuade people to emigrate to?

.... [1]

b) Give two examples of how these posters are similar.

....

.... [2]

c) Give two examples of how these posters are different.

....

.... [2]

d) 'Both posters tell us as much about life in Britain in the 19th century and the 1950s as they do about life in Australia.' Do you agree with this statement?

....

.... [3]

e) Give two examples of other countries people from Britain emigrated to in the 20th century. .... [2]

Total Marks .... / 33

The Kingdom of Benin

1 Study Sources A and B and then answer the questions that follow.

Source A: An oral recollection of the arrival of the Portuguese in Benin, written in the 1890s, showing the developing relationship between Benin and the white traders

> This is how the white men came to Benin. King Esige [Esige was king 1505–c1550] ... sent messengers with some tusks as presents to the country by the big water [the Benin River] where the white men used to come to trade, and they told the messengers to go and salute any white man they found there and beg them to come; which they did, and ever since then white men have come to Benin. The white men stayed long, many many years they came to trade, and if a man comes to trade he must sit down and sell his things softly softly; they used to buy ivory, redwood, oil, gum, and slaves; then there was a different white man who used to come, but he only bought slaves ... These white men ... built houses, big houses with big doors in which they kept their goods and slaves.

Source B: Extract from the writings of Olfert Dapper about Benin, 1686, *Description l'Afrique*

> No one has the right to buy anything from Europeans except the merchants whom the King has appointed ... The goods which the Dutch bring are: cloth of gold and silver; red and scarlet cloth; drinking vessel with red stripes round the mouth; all kinds of fine cotton; linen; candied oranges, lemons and other green fruit; red velvet; brass bracelets; lavender; violet embroidery silk; coarse flannel; fine coral; Harlem fabrics; red glass earrings, mirrors; iron bars; crystal beads; Indian cowries which serve as local currency. The goods which the Dutch take in exchange are: striped cotton garments which are retailed on the Gold Coast, and blue cloths which are sold on the rivers of Gabon and Angola; jasper stones; female slaves, for they refuse to sell men; leopard skins; pepper; and Acori which is a kind of blue coral.

a) According to Source A, why did Europeans first go to Benin?

_____

_____ **[2]**

b) Name three goods that the Europeans bought from Benin.

_____ **[3]**

c) Name three goods that the Europeans sold to Benin.

_____ [3]

d) According to Source B, where did the Europeans sell these goods?

_____ [1]

e) Source A is an oral account of the history of Benin, written down in the 1890s.
How does that affect its value to a historian?

_____

_____

_____ [3]

f) Source B was written by Olfert Dapper, a Dutchman, who may have visited Benin,
although it is more likely he obtained his information from returning sailors.
How does that affect its value to a historian?

_____

_____

_____ [3]

g) 'Both these sources tell us that Benin in the 17th century was a very rich and
powerful empire.' Do you agree?

_____

_____

_____ [3]

Total Marks _____ / 18

World History

Qing China

1 Study Source A and then answer the questions that follow.

Source A: A modern historian writes about the Opium Wars in China

An Opium War was fought between China and Great Britain from 1839 to 1842. Britain wanted to be able to sell Indian opium to China in exchange for tea. The Chinese rulers didn't want the opium. Britain won. There was a second Opium War, from 1856 to 1860, in which France joined Britain. China was defeated again. The terms of China's defeat were harsh: it had to give Hong Kong to Britain until 1999 and had to set up special ports to trade with foreigners, and grant special rights to foreigners living there – the Chinese could not make the laws in these ports, foreigners did. The Chinese government could do nothing whilst the British sold more and more opium to the people of China. The British did this in the name of free trade.

a) Who was fighting the Opium Wars?

.... **[2]**

b) Who won?

.... **[1]**

c) What were the outcomes for Britain?

....

....

....

.... **[3]**

d) What were the consequences for China?

....

....

....

.... **[3]**

2 What do the Opium Wars tell us about the relationship between European powers and China in the middle of the 19th century?

[1]

3 Why was China so weak in the middle of the 19th century?

[3]

4 Who, in your opinion, was mostly to blame for China's weaknesses – Britain or China?

[3]

5 What does the story of blue porcelain tell us about the relationship between China and the West?

[6]

Total Marks / 22

> **Mughal India**

1 Study Sources A and B and then answer the questions that follow.

Source A: Painting of Akbar, dating from the 17th century

Source B: A modern historian writes about Akbar

> Akbar ruled Mughal India for 49 years. His ferocious army tripled the size of the Empire. He ran the country efficiently, and the economy was strong. He set up schools, improved roads and promoted religious tolerance. He made the Hajj to Mecca. Despite being unable to read and write, he had a library of 24 000 volumes. His reign is regarded as a high spot of culture and learning. Yet if he was crossed he was totally ruthless.

a) Do you think Source A is an accurate likeness of Akbar? Explain your answer.

....

....

....   [3]

b) What does the author of Source B think was Akbar's greatest achievement?

.... **[1]**

c) Which source do you think helps us to understand Akbar best? Why?

....

....

.... **[3]**

d) Many historians call Akbar the greatest Mughal Emperor. Do you think he deserves to be called Akbar the Great?

....

....

.... **[3]**

2 Muslims and Hindus in Moghul India lived together in peace and harmony. How does this compare with religious ideas in Tudor England under Edward VI, Mary and Elizabeth?

....

....

....

.... **[4]**

3 The Taj Mahal is a World Heritage Site. World Heritage Sites are designated by UNESCO for having cultural, historical, scientific or other significance. According to World Heritage UK, UNESCO 'seeks to encourage the identification, protection and preservation of cultural and natural heritage around the world considered to be of outstanding value to humanity'. Over 1100 sites, in 167 countries, have been made World Heritage Sites. Do you think the Taj Mahal deserves to be a World Heritage Site? Why?

....

....

....

.... **[3]**

Total Marks .... **/ 17**

World History

The West Indies: Fighting Back Against Slavery

1 Read Source A and use the information in the source and in the supplied bullets to complete the timeline on the next page by writing the correct letters in each box. **[10]**

Source A: The Haitian Revolution

In 1789, 550 000 people lived in Saint-Domingue, the country we now call Haiti – 500 000 of them were slaves. It was a rich colony, producing 40 per cent of Europe's sugar and 60 per cent of its coffee. By 1791, it was the richest sugar island in the Caribbean. When the French gave citizenship to 'all people of colour' if they were wealthy enough in 1791, Toussaint L' Ouverture – a free black man – led a revolt demanding the end of slavery and independence for the country. They defeated the French settlers and set up their own government, led by Toussaint. He was a strong leader and respected by all. European countries were worried that other colonies would copy Saint-Domingue and revolt against slavery and colonialism. In 1801, Napoleon sent a French army to reconquer the island, reintroduce slavery and capture Toussaint. Thousands of French soldiers died of disease, especially yellow fever, and the invasion failed, partly because of the rebel army and its guerrilla tactics. The French did, however, capture Toussaint and take him as a prisoner to France where he died in 1803. Dessalines, one of Toussaint's generals, completed the victory and, in 1804, Saint-Domingue became an independent country, the first in the Caribbean, and the first nation to be founded by former slaves. Some historians have called the revolt 'the most significant uprising of enslaved people in history' and it encouraged other rebellions in the Caribbean.

A   The French Government abolishes slavery

B   Toussaint dies in a French prison

C   Toussaint leads the first rebellion against slave owners

D   Toussaint's forces control the whole island

E   The rebels control 33 per cent of the island

F   Britain ends the slave trade

G   French Government gives 'full citizenship to people of colour' (if wealthy enough)

H   Haiti declares itself an independent country

I   French troops invade Haiti, capture Toussaint and take him to France as a prisoner

J   French troops defeated

Toussaint L'Ouverture

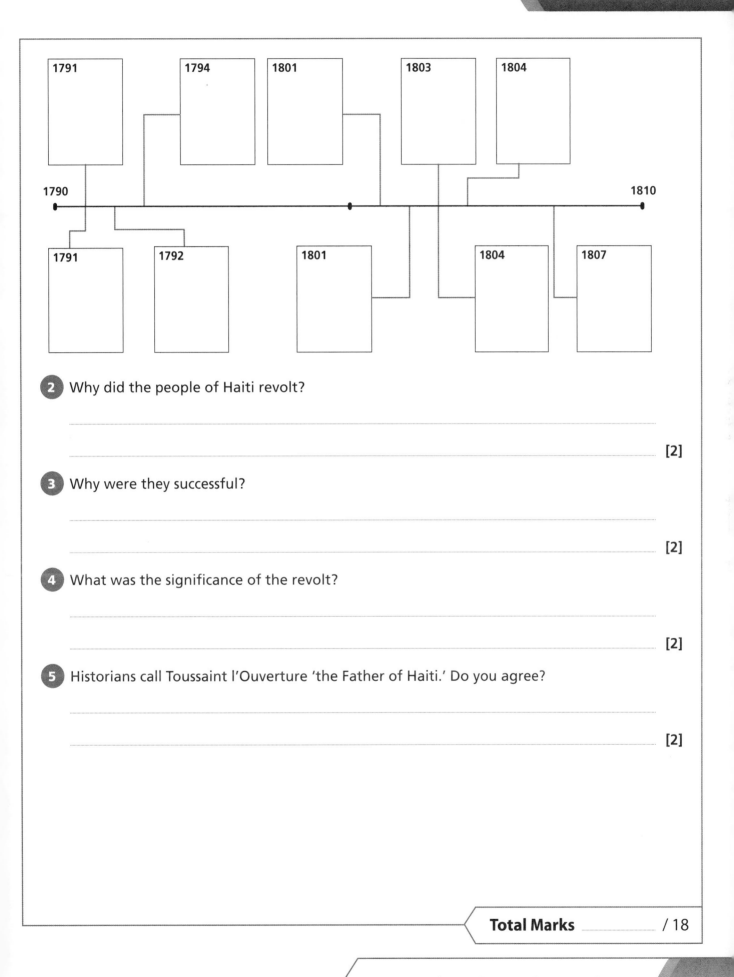

1791	1794	1801	1803	1804

1790   1810

1791	1792	1801	1804	1807

2 Why did the people of Haiti revolt?

....

.... [2]

3 Why were they successful?

....

.... [2]

4 What was the significance of the revolt?

....

.... [2]

5 Historians call Toussaint l'Ouverture 'the Father of Haiti.' Do you agree?

....

.... [2]

Total Marks .... / 18

Mixed Test-Style Questions

Choose just one question to answer. Each question is worth 5 marks.

1 Study the following source from a speech made by John Lilburne in 1647.

> All and every particular and individual man and woman, that ever breathed in the world,
> are by nature all equal and alike in their power, dignity, authority and majesty, none of them
> having (by nature) any authority, dominion or magisterial power one over or above another.

What useful information does this source give us about the tensions in England before and during the English Civil Wars? What are its drawbacks? Give reasons for your answer.

2 Study the following source, published in 1731, which is an extract from the writings of Khafi Khan (1664–1732) who was a civil servant and historian of Mughal India.

> Akbar was pre-eminent as a conqueror and law-giver, yet for the order and arrangement of
> his territory and finances and good administration of every department of the state, no prince
> ever reigned in India that could be compared to Shah Jahan.

What useful information does the source give you about the Mughal rulers, Akbar and Shah Jahan? Why is this not enough evidence to decide whether Akbar or Shah Jahan were the greatest rulers of Mughal India? Give reasons for your answer.

Mixed Test-Style Questions

Choose just one question to answer. Each question is worth 5 marks.

1 Study the following source which is an advert for a sea voyage.

What does this source definitely tell us about the voyage? What does it probably tell us about the voyage? What do we still need to find out about the voyage?

2 Study the following source by Sophia Jex-Blake, one of six female medical students at the University of Edinburgh in the late 1800s, which describes events in Edinburgh in November 1870.

> On the afternoon of Friday 18th November 1870, we walked to the Surgeon's Hall, where the anatomy examination was to be held. As soon as we reached the Surgeon's Hall we saw a dense mob filling up the road... The crowd was sufficient to stop all the traffic for an hour. We walked up to the gates, which remained open until we came within a yard of them, when they were slammed in our faces by a number of young men.

How useful is this source in telling us about the problems women faced in training as doctors in Victorian times? Give reasons for your answer.

Mixed Test-Style Questions

Choose just one question to answer. Each question is worth 5 marks.

1 Study the source below which is an extract from Correlli Barnett's 2003 book about World War I, *The Great War*.

> For the majority of soldiers actual living conditions in and behind the lines on quiet sectors were little, if any, worse, than in peacetime. Certainly many British soldiers enjoyed a better diet, better medical care and better welfare than they had as civilians.

What information would you need to decide whether Correlli Barnett's assessment is correct?

2 Read the following source from a sermon by John Ball given at Blackheath as the peasants waited to meet King Richard III on 12 June 1381.

> When Adam delved, and Eve span, who was then the gentleman? From the beginning all men by nature were created alike, and our bondage or servitude came in by the unjust oppression of naughty men.

How useful is this source in explaining the causes, events and consequences of the Peasants' Revolt? Give reasons for your answer.

Mixed Test-Style Questions

Choose just one question to answer. Each question is worth 5 marks.

1 During the Second World War, the British and American governments decided to develop an atom bomb – a 'super weapon' – that might end the war quicker, and with less loss of life of Allied soldiers. By summer 1945, the atom bomb was ready for use. Read the following source from a report by the US Scientific Panel dated 16 June 1945.

> The opinions of our scientific colleagues on the initial use of these weapons are not unanimous: they range from the proposal of a purely technical demonstration to that of the military application best designed to induce surrender. Those who advocate a purely technical demonstration would wish to outlaw the use of atomic weapons, and have feared that if we use the weapons now our position in future negotiations will be prejudiced. Others emphasize the opportunity of saving American lives by immediate military use, and believe that such use will improve the international prospects, in that they are more concerned with the prevention of war than with the elimination of this specific weapon. We find ourselves closer to these latter views; we can propose no technical demonstration likely to bring an end to the war; we see no acceptable alternative to direct military use.

How does the provenance and content of this source help us to understand the debate over whether or not to drop the Atom Bomb on Japan in 1945?

2 Look at the source below. It is an extract from an 1831 poster and contains information from the UK Board of Health.

INDIAN CHOLERA

It is deemed proper to call the attention of the Inhabitants to some of the Symptoms and Remedies mentioned by them as printed, and now in circulation.

Symptoms of the Disorder;

Giddiness, sickness, nervous agitation, slow pulse, cramp beginning at the fingers and toes and rapidly approaching the trunk, change of colour to a leaden blue, purple, black or brown; the skin dreadfully cold, and often damp, the tongue moist and loaded but flabby and chilly, the voice much affected, and respiration quick and irregular.

REMEDIES;

All means tending to restore circulation and to maintain the warmth of the body should be had recourse to without the least delay.

The patient should be immediately put to bed, wrapped up in hot blankets, and warmth should be sustained by other external applications, such as repeated frictions with flannels and camphorated spirits, poultices of mustard and linseed (equal parts) to the stomach, particularly where pain and vomiting exist, and similar poultices to the feet and legs to restore their warmth. The returning heat of the body may be promoted by bags containing hot salt or bran applied to different parts, and for the same purpose of restoring and sustaining the circulation white wine wey with spice, hot brandy and water, or salvolatile in a dose of a tea spoon full in hot water, frequently repeated; or from 5 to 20 drops of some of the essential oils, as peppermint, cloves or cajeput, in a wine glass of water may be administered with the same view. Where the stomach will bear it, warm broth with spice may be employed. In every severe case or where medical aid is difficult to be obtained, from 20 to 40 drops of laudanum may be given in any of the warm drinks previously recommended.

These simple means are proposed as resources in the incipient stages of the Disease, until Medical aid can be had.

What does this source tell you about the Government's response to the cholera epidemic of 1831–32?

Mixed Test-Style Questions

Choose just one question to answer. Each question is worth 10 marks.

1 How did the design and function of castles change during the Middle Ages? Support your answer with evidence.

2 Imagine you are a peasant in Norman England. Write an account of your life across a year. In your answer you should highlight some of the main difficulties you face.

3 Describe the battle of Marston Moor in 1644, explaining why the Parliamentarian Army won.

Mixed Test-Style Questions

Choose just one question to answer. Each question is worth 10 marks.

1 Look at the following diagram.

Is it accurate to talk about the 'Triangular Trade'? Support your answer with evidence.

2 'The railways really did make the world smaller.' Do you agree? Use examples to support your answer.

3 'The assassination of Archduke Franz Ferdinand in Sarajevo on 28 June 1914 was the real cause of the First World War.' Do you agree? Use evidence to support your answer.

Mixed Test-Style Questions

Choose just one question to answer. Each question is worth 10 marks.

1. Explain the most important reason for the success of D-Day. In your answer you should explain different reasons for its success and then decide which reason you think is most important.

2. The development of the Welfare State is regarded as a major breakthrough in the health and wellbeing of ordinary people. Give your opinion as to why it is so important.

3. Explain why the 1960s is known as 'the Swinging Sixties'. In your answer you should explore at least three major changes in the 1960s and say if you think the title is appropriate.

Mixed Test-Style Questions

Choose just one question to answer. Each question is worth 10 marks.

1 Why did Benin abolish the slave trade in 1530 and then re-introduce it in 1730? Support your answer with evidence.

2 In your opinion, why did the British come to an agreement with the Maroons, rather than defeat them?

3 What can we learn about women's fight for the vote from the work of Sophia Duleep Singh, daughter of the Maharajah of Punjab?

THIS PAGE HAS DELIBERATELY BEEN LEFT BLANK

Answers

The Norman Conquest

1. a) Harthacnut, a Viking King of England from 1040–1042, had promised the throne to Hardrada's father, Magnus; when his father died, Hardrada claimed the throne himself. **[2]**
   b) William claimed his cousin, Edward, who had no children, had promised him the throne in 1051; the Pope supported his claim. **[2]**
   c) Harold was the most powerful earl in England and had mostly run the country for the last few years; the Anglo-Saxons had chosen him as King when Edward died; he claimed Edward had promised him the throne on his deathbed; he was the only Anglo-Saxon claiming the throne. **[2]**
   d) Any suitable answer, supported by reasons. One mark for each valid point made up to a maximum of two. **[2]**
   e) One mark for each valid point made up to a maximum of three, e.g. he had the strongest army; Harold was killed; the Anglo-Saxons had already marched over 600km to Stamford Bridge and back, and fought a battle against Harald; the Normans played a trick and pretended to retreat; William had rested his men the night before the battle. **[3]**
2. a) Countess Judith **[1]**
   b) 3½ hides (1 hide = 120 acres) **[1]**
   c) 29 (14 villagers, 11 smallholders, 4 slaves) **[1]**
   d) £10 in 1066 **[1]** and 100 shillings (£5) in 1086 **[1] [2]**
   e) It could be used to grind corn into flour **[1]**, which would be a source of income for the Lord **[1]**. **[2]**
   f) To find out who owned the land **[1]**; to find out how wealthy England was **[1]**; to help decide what taxes he was due **[1]**. **[3]**
   g) Any suitable answer, supported by reasons. One mark for each valid point made up to a maximum of five, e.g. Strengths: it tells us who owned the land and how wealthy England was; it was compiled by the King's officials; it was checked. Weaknesses: it doesn't cover every village in the country; people might have lied about their wealth so as to pay less tax; the officials might have got things wrong. **[5]**

Christendom and the Crusades

1. a) The chapel/church **[1]** – it is by far the largest building and dominates the site **[1]**. **[2]**
   b) Provided medical help – there is a hospital **[1]**; provided accommodation – there is a guesthouse **[1]**; copied books – there is a scriptorium **[1]**. **[3]**
   c) People who were not monks **[1]** but who lived and worked at the monastery **[1]**. **[2]**
   d) People gave land and money to the Church as a way to get to heaven when they died (indulgences) and had to pay a tithe of 10 per cent of their earnings to the Church **[1]**; most monks could read and write so had an important part to play in running the country and were rewarded for their work **[1]**. **[2]**
   e) Any two of: to devote their lives to God; monasteries were a safe place to live and work; to obtain an education; it represented a chance to get a better job; to get power – the abbot was a powerful man. **[2]**
2. a) Who had the most power – Church or King **[1]**. Henry wanted less power for the Church courts **[1]**,

Thomas believed the King had no authority to limit the Church's power **[1]**. **[3]**
   b) Any suitable answer, supported by reasons. One mark for each valid point made up to a maximum of three, e.g. Very: it shows us the knights killing Thomas; it supports the eye-witness account of the priest Edward Grim; it tells us what Victorians thought happened. Not very: it was drawn much later; it only tells part of the story. **[3]**
   c) Any suitable answer, supported by reasons. One mark for each valid point made up to a maximum of two, e.g. Source A – secondary; historian; studied events; weighed up the evidence. Source B – secondary; based on an eye-witness account. **[2]**

Magna Carta

1. a) John fought with his brother against his father for control of England. **[1]**
   b) When Richard was on his Crusade, John set himself up as ruler **[1]**; John told people Richard was dead and he, John, should be king **[1]**. **[2]**
   c) Any two of: he was strong-willed and ambitious; he had a temper; he was greedy; he was devious. **[2]**
   d) Any suitable answer, supported by reasons. One mark for each valid point made up to a maximum of four, e.g. Yes – he argued with the Pope over the choosing of the Archbishop; the Pope removed the rights of priests and bishops to conduct services in England; he was a weak leader who lost land in Ireland and Europe; he put up taxes again and again; people who were rich could escape justice by paying John money; he was very cruel; he killed Arthur, who had a claim to the throne; he forced himself on the wives and daughters of his friends – no one was safe from him. No – he was a good administrator; he ran the country well; he was cautious with his army and avoided battle if he could, rather than being a coward who refused to fight; he took over a country ruined by Richard's wars and spending and absences; he stayed in England to rule. **[4]**
2. a) To raise taxes **[1]**; to gather support for Simon de Montfort **[1]**. **[2]**
   b) It was formed by people other than lords and churchmen for the first time. **[1]**
   c) The House of Lords was made up of barons and senior churchmen as before **[1]** but the House of Commons was made up of two knights from each shire **[1]** and two burgesses (**citizens**) from the main towns and cities **[1]** who were elected **[1]**. **[4]**
   d) Any suitable answer, supported by reasons. One mark for each valid point made up to a maximum of three, e.g. Similar: consisted of the House of Lords and the House of Commons; dealt with taxes. Different: the House of Commons is now much more important than Lords; power – it makes laws, runs the country; the monarch can advise government but not insist; House of Lords has less power. **[3]**

The Black Death

1. a) One mark for each valid point made up to a maximum of three, e.g. placed dried flowers and herbs over their nose and mouth to protect against the bad air;

lit fires to destroy the bad air; used dried toads and leeches to remove poison from the body; rubbed raw onion, butter and figs on the lumps to soften and reduce them; rubbed vinegar on their bodies or drank it to stop them catching it; prayed; isolated themselves; doctors took blood from sick patients. **[3]**

   b) No – because no one understood the cause, it was very difficult to find an effective treatment. **[1]**

   c) Isolated victims in their own homes; cleared the streets of rubbish; lit fires to disperse the bad air that they thought spread the disease. **[3]**

   d) It encouraged people to pray every day; attend church; engage in flagellation. **[3]**

2. a) Any logical order is correct, although some effects, like prices and wages going up, might seem more important than others. **[1]**

   b) Answers will vary depending on the response to part a). One mark for each of three points made, e.g. 'It was easier for a lower-class person to improve their wealth...' is most important because it meant that people were no longer so restricted in what they could do and what they could earn. **[3]**

   c) Answers will vary depending on the response to part a). One mark for each of three points made, e.g. 'many houses collapsed...' is least important because they were no longer needed as there were fewer people in towns and villages. **[3]**

   d) It became less virulent over the winter of 1349, and by 1350 things seemed to be returning to normal, but it kept returning over the next 300 years. **[1]**

Pages 156–157

The Peasants' Revolt

1. a)

	Long	Medium	Short
The Poll Taxes of 1377, 1379 and 1380			✓
Resentment of peasants at having to work two or three days a week for their lords	✓		
The preaching of John Ball		✓	
Richard II was a new, young and inexperienced king		✓	
The Black Death	✓		
The Statute of Labourers 1351	✓		
England doing badly in the Hundred Years War and increasing French attacks in the South and East		✓	
The attempt to collect unpaid Poll Tax in Fobbing, Essex, on 30 May 1381			✓
The feudal system	✓		

[9]

   b) Any sensible answer with logical support. One mark for each of two points made, e.g. the Poll Taxes were most important because poor people thought it unfair that rich and poor had to pay the same tax. **[2]**

   c) Any sensible answer with logical support. One mark for each of two points made, e.g. Richard II was the least important because he didn't have a direct impact on a lot of the population. **[2]**

   d) Any sensible answer with logical support. One mark for each of two points made, e.g. 1381 when officials collected the tax and it was clear nothing would change for the poorer people. **[2]**

2. a) Black Death; Statute of Labourers; Poll Tax introduced; Attempt to collect Poll Tax in Fobbing; Peasants march on London; Richard II tries to speak to the peasants; Richard II speaks to the peasants at Mile End; Wat Tyler meets the King and is killed by the Mayor of London; Richard II promises the peasants he will meet all their demands; Peasants go home; Richard II sets the army on any rebels; Many rebels killed **[12]**

   b) Any answer is acceptable, with supporting detail, e.g. Wat Tyler – leader of the peasants, spokesman, organiser; John Ball – preacher, his ideas of equality; Richard II – brave, met the rebels, lied to them, killed many rebels, kept the peace AND his kingship. One mark for each of three points made. **[3]**

Pages 158–159

Reformation and Counter-Reformation

1. Any two of: he broke away from the Church in Rome; every church had to have a copy of the Bible in English; church services were in English not Latin; Henry rather than the Pope appointed bishops. **[2]**

2. Any two of: allowed priests to marry; introduced a new prayer book; Mass was replaced by Holy Communion – a much simpler service; statues and paintings were removed from churches. **[2]**

3. Any two of: Mass was brought back; the Pope was made head of the Church again; Protestant bishops were removed and replaced with Catholic ones. **[2]**

4. Any suitable answer, supported by reasons. One mark for each valid point made up to a maximum of four, e.g. Henry VIII because he started it all off, set up the Church of England and removed the power of the pope; without that, none of the other changes could have happened. **[4]**

5. One mark for each valid point made, up to a maximum of four, e.g. Henry wanted a divorce which the Catholic Church wouldn't allow so he broke away from the Roman Church; Edward wanted the Church to be more Protestant; Mary wanted the Church to return to the Catholic faith; Henry and Edward wanted to run the country and felt the Pope was stopping that; new ideas changed the way some people thought about the Church; some people felt the Church was out of touch with ordinary people. **[4]**

6. Example answers follow but other answers are possible.

   a) In Source A there are more decorations **[1]** and more statues and religious objects **[1]** than there are in Source B. **[2]**

   b) There is an aisle **[1]** an altar **[1]**, and a cross **[1]** in both sources. **[3]**

   c) There would be fewer Catholics **[1]** because people would be more likely to attend a Protestant church **[1]**. Or, the churches would have less money **[1]** as they did not have as many expensive statues and furnishings **[1]**. Or there would be a further divide between Catholics and protestants in England **[1]** leading to more unrest in the community **[1]**. **[2]**

Pages 160–161

The English Civil Wars

1. August 1642 **[1]**

2. January 1649, when the King was executed **[1]**

3. One mark for each valid point made, up to a maximum of three, e.g. He was seen as arrogant and believed in the 'Divine Right of Kings'; he ruled for 11 years without Parliament; people thought he was about to turn England Catholic again (his wife was a Catholic); his wars meant he needed lots of money – he raised taxes without asking Parliament; he attempted to arrest five Members of Parliament who refused to give in to his demands. **[3]**
4. One mark for each valid point made, up to a maximum of three, e.g. MPs wanted a bigger say in running the country; they wanted Charles to let Parliament control the army; many of them wanted religion to be more Protestant; they hated the Ship Tax; they used his argument with the Scots to win more influence. **[3]**
5. Any answer is acceptable as long as it is supported by reasons, based on your answers to the previous questions. One mark for each of two points made, e.g. the King because he chose to rule alone, refused to listen to Parliament and didn't grant Parliament its requests. **[2]**
6. a) Musketeer **[1]**; a musket (one shot, long time to reload) **[1]**; he was directly responsible for killing the enemy **[1]**. **[3]**
    b) Pikeman **[1]**; a five-metre pike **[1]**; he protected the musketeers from a cavalry charge **[1]**. **[3]**
    c) Cavalry **[1]**; pistol and sword **[1]**; he would break though the enemy line **[1]**. **[3]**
    d) Any three of: set up in 1645 by Parliament; could be ordered to serve anywhere in the country; its leaders could not serve in Parliament; the soldiers were full-time and paid; many held very strong religious views; people were promoted on ability not birth status; it was a very disciplined army. **[3]**

Pages 162–163

The Interregnum

1. Any four of: theatres were all closed down; pubs and ale-houses were restricted; dancing, bear-baiting and other sports were banned; Christmas and Easter festivities were outlawed; people were urged to live a simple and moral life; taxes went up. **[4]**
2. Some did, especially Puritans, who believed in a simple life and loved the changes **[1]**. Many found them too restrictive which made Cromwell unpopular **[1]**. **[2]**
3. Similar – any two of: leader for life; had great power – could dissolve Parliament and veto bills; worked with Parliament. Different – any two of: leader of a republic, not a monarchy; elected not hereditary, even if he could choose his successor; no crown. **[4]**
4. a) The Merry Monarch **[1]**
    b) Because he loved life and wanted to have fun **[1]**. He enjoyed parties, wine and horse racing, and had many mistresses **[1]**. **[2]**
5. Any three of: to avoid a political crisis; Cromwell had become unpopular and was seen as greedy; when Cromwell died, his son took over but he was not up to the job and resigned in 1659; the former Parliament was recalled which supported the monarchy; people wanted stability; Charles promised to be a 'good king' (by implication, not like his father). **[3]**
6. Any three of: only members of the Church of England could be MPs, teachers or priests; he restored the House of Lords; he restored land to those who had lost it fighting for the King during the Civil War; he removed all the restrictions Cromwell had introduced. **[3]**

Pages 164–165

Transatlantic Slave Trade/Abolition of the Slave Trade

1. To work on the plantations that were growing cotton, sugar and tobacco that Europeans wanted to buy. **[1]**
2. They thought Africans were physiologically different and were uncivilised, and only suited to hard labour. **[1]**
3. One mark for each valid point made, up to a maximum of three, e.g. brutal – hard work; long hours; no control over your own life; sold away from family; subject to harsh punishments. **[3]**
4. Any three of: white anti-slavery campaigners such as Sharp and Clarkson; freed black people like Equiano and Mary Prince; many Quakers; some ex-slavers (captains/owners of the ships taking slaves to the Americas) like John Newton and Alexander Falconbridge; some MPs; some consumers of sugar who boycotted it. **[3]**
5. Any two of: plantation owners; slave owners in Britain and in the Caribbean; traders in Britain such as Edward Colston; factory owners in Britain who were dependent on the raw materials produced by slaves; dock workers in Britain whose jobs depended on slavery. **[2]**
6. The 1833 Slavery Abolition Act made it illegal to own slaves in most of the British Empire. **[1]**
7. 1865, after the American Civil War. **[1]**
8. 1948 **[1]**; no – illegal slavery continues around the world **[1]**. **[2]**
9. a) They still had a workforce, but had to pay them **[1]**; they charged rent for houses **[1]**; they received compensation from the British Government (£20 million in total) **[1]**. **[3]**
    b) Same jobs, same places **[1]**; few political rights **[1]**; unless they left the plantations and went to live in the unsettled lands **[1]**. **[3]**
    c) Any suitable answer, supported by reasons. One mark for each valid point made up to a maximum of two, e.g. Useful: it shows little had changed – the plantation owners still dominated society, the economy and life; Not very useful: it only tells us what happened immediately after abolition, not what happened in subsequent years. **[2]**

Pages 166–167

Britain as the First Industrial Nation

1. Sir Richard Arkwright **[1]**
2. By water wheels **[1]**
3. a) Any suitable answer, supported by reasons. One mark for each valid point made up to a maximum of two, e.g. yes, he describes how he disliked spending money, although this might be from newspaper stories about Arkwright. **[2]**
    b) Any suitable answer, supported by reasons. One mark for each valid point made up to a maximum of two, e.g. yes, he describes him as a 'genius' **[1]** and refers to his good work making the country richer; not sure – he describes him as a 'useful person' but he's not really described in a likeable way **[1]**. **[2]**
    c) Lucky **[1]** – he was in the right place at the right time and bought the invention for £50 **[1]** but also a successful entrepreneur **[1]** who made a lot of money and provided jobs **[1]**. **[4]**
4. a) Any three of: He describes him as a brilliant entrepreneur who started the Industrial Revolution **[1]**; he clearly admires him **[1]** using words like 'genius' and 'creator' and saying he 'transformed England' **[1]**; he implies he was a good man because he built houses for workers and a school and church **[1]**. **[3]**

b) He says he made him work long hours and turned him into a cripple [1]. It is unlikely he liked him [1] – he doesn't say specifically, but we can infer it from what he says when he describes his work making him 'a miserable cripple' and talks of being 'cast off … without a single penny' [1]. [3]

c) They are talking about different things [1] – the historian is examining Arkwright's impact on the country as a whole and his legacy [1], while John Reed is describing his personal experience of working in the factory [1]; together, they build up a bigger picture [1] of the Industrial Revolution benefiting the owners but not the workers [1]. [5]

Pages 168–169

Democratic Reform

1. More men could vote if they owned property (but still only about 25 per cent) [1]; rotten boroughs were abolished [1]; some new industrial towns and cities now had their own MPs [1]. [3]

2. a) Any suitable answer, supported by reasons. One mark for each valid point made up to a maximum of two, e.g. a vote for every man over 21 is most important as it would allow men to influence laws and get a decent wage. [2]

   b) Any suitable answer, supported by reasons. One mark for each valid point made up to a maximum of two, e.g. equal constituencies is least important because it doesn't matter as much if everybody can vote. [2]

   c) Any suitable answer, supported by reasons. One mark for each valid point made up to a maximum of three, e.g. too radical; thought they had made enough changes; didn't really want democracy; thought the chartists wanted a revolution. [3]

3. Skilled male workers in towns could vote [1]; people who rented property worth £10 a year or more instead of owning it could vote [1]; increased the number of men who could vote to 2.5 million [1]. [3]

4. The secret ballot was introduced [1] to deal with problems of corruption, bribery and intimidation [1]; men could now vote without their employer or landlord knowing who they had voted for [1]. [3]

5. More men could vote – six million were now eligible, or nearly 66 per cent of all men; constituencies now only had one MP [1]; towns and the countryside were treated the same way [1]. [3]

6. Any suitable answer with supporting reasons, based on the answers above. One mark for each of four points made. [4]

7. No – most men could vote but no women [1]; it was becoming more democratic, but still only 18 per cent of the population could vote [1]. [2]

Pages 170–171

Women's Suffrage

1. Keep their own property when they married [1]; Keep their own income when they married [1]; Vote in a general election [1] [3]

2. Vote in a general election [1]

3. Vote in a general election [1]

4. Any three of: Their fathers or husbands should look after them; women were the 'weaker' sex and unable to run their own affairs; many people thought a woman's job was in the home/bringing up children; some wealthy women, including Queen Victoria, opposed rights for women. [3]

5. In 1867 with the Parliamentary Reform Act – it failed. [1]

6. a) 1872 [1]

   b) Not very [1] – after 1870, a vote on women's suffrage took place in Parliament every year, to no avail [1]. [2]

7. a) The National Union of Women's Suffrage Societies (NUWSS) [1]

   b) They wanted the vote on the same terms as men – middle-class property-owning or renting women [1]. They believed in persuasion [1] to show that women were responsible enough to be given the vote [1] and used peaceful tactics [1] such as lobbying MPs, holding peaceful demonstrations and petitions [1]. [5]

   c) Not very [1]. Because they believed in peaceful methods, and the vote for wealthy women, they didn't get very much support [1]. [2]

8. a)

Similar to NUWSS	Different to NUWSS
Wanted the vote for all women	Used violent tactics
Made up of middle-class and working-class women	Disrupted political meetings
	Went on hunger strike when sent to prison

[5]

   b) Any suitable answer, supported by reasons. One mark for each valid point made up to a maximum of three, e.g. WSPU alienated many and delayed the vote; NUWSS was too timid and thus was not influential; neither – it was the part women played in World War I that persuaded Parliament to give women the vote in 1918. [3]

Pages 172–173

The First World War

1. 28 June 1914 [1], Sarajevo [1] [2]

2. 11 November 1918 [1]

3. New weapons made it easier to defend your own trenches than attack the enemy [1], yet generals sent troops 'over the top' to attack trenches [1]. [2]

4. Any two of: all weapons were coordinated; enemy strong points were avoided; it was a war of movement not static; the lessons of 1914–1917 had been learned; it was carefully planned. [2]

5. a)

Country	Gained	Lost
Britain	✓	
France	✓	
Germany		✓
Austria-Hungary		✓
Turkey (Ottoman Empire)		✓

[5]

   b) Those on the losing side all lost land [1]; those on the winning side all gained land [1] [2]

6. a) In 1919, there are lots of small new countries in the East of Europe [1], such as Poland and Czechoslovakia, which are made out of the old territory of Germany, Austria-Hungary and Turkey [1]. [2]

   b) Any suitable answer, supported by reasons. One mark for each valid point made up to a maximum of three, e.g. Safer – each nation had its own country (e.g., all Poles were in Poland, all Czechs in Czechoslovakia) so there would be no need to fight;

More dangerous – Germany would want to take back the land it had lost, it would want revenge. Also would the small countries (e.g. Estonia, Latvia, Lithuania) be strong enough to stand up to someone invading them? **[3]**

Pages 174–175

The Second World War

1. 30 January 1933 **[1]**. Any two of: to tear up the Treaty of Versailles, to reunify Germany and Austria, to make Germany great again, to gain 'lebensraum' or 'Living Space' for the German people, to show Germany was the Master Race, to destroy Communism. **[3]**
2. May 1937 **[1]**; Appeasement – he believed Germany had some genuine grievances that needed to be dealt with **[1]**; negotiation, as at Munich in 1938, to keep the peace **[1]**. **[3]**
3. 1933 **[1]**; isolationism – Europe's problems were nothing to do with the USA **[1]**. **[2]**
4. October 1917 **[1]**; to spread communism **[1]**. **[2]**
5. Any suitable answer, supported by reasons. One mark for each valid point made up to a maximum of three, e.g. Roosevelt was most important because America's policy of isolation encouraged Hitler in his attempts to take over other countries – he thought no one would try to stop him. **[3]**
6. The belief that bombers would always get through any air defences **[1]** and that bombing could win the war **[1]**. **[2]**
7. a) Cities have been hit by bombs **[1]**; it proves that bombers can drop bombs **[1]** but it doesn't prove that the war could be won by bombing **[1]**. **[3]**
    b) Any suitable answer, supported by reasons. One mark for each valid point made up to a maximum of four, e.g. Very useful: they are primary sources (taken at the time) and show the extent of the damage; they show information that it might be hard to convey through words. Not very useful: they could be propaganda – where selective photos are released only showing part of the damage; we need context to really understand them; don't know who took the photos or why. Conclusion: photos might be useful but need to be used with other evidence. **[4]**

Pages 176–177

The Creation of the Welfare State

1. **1906** Free School meals introduced; **1907** School Medical Inspectors introduced; **1908** Old Age pensions introduced; **1909** Labour Exchanges set up; **1911** National Insurance Act; **1942** Beveridge Report published; **1948** NHS set up; **1951** Prescription charge introduced **[8]**
2. Because they thought they would lose money if they were not able to treat private patients. **[1]**
3. Everyone could afford to see a doctor/optician/dentist because it was free **[1]**; people were healthier/lived longer **[1]**; many dangerous diseases like polio were eradicated **[1]**. **[3]**
4. Want; Disease; Squalor; Ignorance; Idleness **[5]**
5. a) Reforms to benefits **[1]** mean those out of work or on low pay need to rely on food banks to eat **[1]**. **[2]**
    b) To put pressure on the Government to change its policies. **[1]**
    c) Any suitable answer, supported by reasons. One mark for each valid point made up to a maximum of four, e.g. Very useful: it tells us that many people in 2013 relied on benefits and didn't have enough

to eat **[1]**; it tells us what Church Action on Poverty thinks **[1]**; it tells us that some people feel there is too much poverty **[1]**. Not so useful: it is only part of the picture **[1]**; it is meant to persuade people to do something **[1]**; it only addresses hunger/not enough to eat – it doesn't tell us about health care, housing or education **[1]**. Overall: it gives us primary evidence for some aspects of the Welfare State in 2013 **[1]**. **[4]**

Pages 178–179

Britain's Place in the Word 1945–Present

1. Any two, e.g.: food rationing ended; commerical television started; immigrants started coming to Britain to fill vacant jobs; polio vaccine introduced; first space flights. **[2]**
2. Any two e.g.: abortion and homosexuality made legal; contraceptive pill freely available; women's roles in society started changing; over 80 per cent of households had a television; teenage culture developed; 'Swinging Sixties'; racial discrimination made illegal. **[2]**
3. Any two e.g.: most houses had private indoor bathrooms; central heating in most homes; Britain joined the EEC; many strikes over pay; many British people emigrated to Australia and New Zealand; a lot of British factories closed and unemployment increased; coal miners' strike – many pits closed; decimal currency introduced; the digital watch was invented; voting age was lowered to 18. **[2]**
4. Any two e.g.: most homes had fridges and freezers; colour television ownership was widespread; privatisation of many industries like gas and electric; microwave ovens widely available. **[2]**
5. Any two e.g.: more people became self-employed; growth of the internet; spread of satellite television; first mobile phones. **[2]**
6. Answers will vary. Answers should be supported with evidence from above – it is the quality of supporting argument that is important. One mark for each of four points made. **[4]**
7. 1979 **[1]**
8. a) Any three of: crushed the trade unions; privatisation; tax cuts; more productive economy; long overdue reforms. **[3]**
    b) Wiped out lots of industry; wasted the money from North Sea oil; made the country more unequal **[3]**
    c) Because many benefitted and became richer as a result of tax cuts and growth in some areas like banking **[1]**, while many others suffered because of policies that destroyed old industries **[1]**. **[2]**
9. Any suitable answer, supported by reasons. One mark for each valid point made up to a maximum of four, e.g. Yes: society, especially politics, was still very sexist; she 'broke the glass ceiling' and now we have many more female MPs; it is one thing about her that people can agree on. No: she created great changes in Britain – although not all positive. **[4]**

Pages 180–181

Migration To and From the British Isles

1.

Push factor	Pull factor
war	better education opportunities
unemployment	better standard of living
poverty	plenty of jobs available
lack of opportunity	better housing

[8]

2. Soldiers in the Roman army; Anglo-Saxons; Vikings; Normans; Huguenots; Irish; Jewish migrants from Russia and Poland; Caribbean migrants; Commonwealth citizens from Asia; citizens of the EU [10]

3. Any five of: created a multicultural society; wider range of food and restaurants available; helped fill available jobs; taken the jobs no one else wants; cultural events such as Notting Hill Carnival; changed people's attitudes (made people more – or less – racist); sometimes increased tensions in society; played a part in politics; population growth; increase in different religious beliefs and places of worship; brought in many skilled workers; boosted the economy; introduced new fashions and music; any other reasonable impact. [5]

4. a) Australia [1]
   b) Any two similarities, e.g. they encourage people to move to Australia; they offer jobs; they target people who are out of work/dissatisfied in Britain. [2]
   c) Any two of: 1950s poster talks about a better place to live as well as work; adults have to pay £10 to go to Australia in the 1950s whereas it was free in the 19th century; the 19th-century poster is issued by Britain's Colonial Office while the 1950s poster was issued by the Government of Australia; the 1950s poster mentions children; the 19th-century poster lists specific trades that are eligible; any other reasonable difference. [2]
   d) Any suitable answer, supported by reasons. One mark for each valid point made up to a maximum of three, e.g. Yes – some people had reasons to leave Britain ('push factors'), such as unemployment, especially among agricultural workers and builders, as well as reasons to go to Australia ('pull factors'), such as a new life, space to live, higher wages and a 40-hour week; they are both primary sources so tell us how authorities at each of these times were encouraging people to migrate to Australia. [3]
   e) Any two of, for example, America, Canada, New Zealand, Kenya, South Africa. [2]

Pages 182–183

The Kingdom of Benin

1. a) They were invited by King Esige [1]; they wanted to trade [1]. [2]
   b) Any three of: ivory, redwood, oil, gum, slaves, garments, jasper stones, female slaves, leopard skins, pepper and acori. [3]
   c) Any three of: fine cotton, linen, candied fruit, red velvet, brass bracelets, lavender, embroidery silk, flannel, coral, fabrics, glass earrings, mirrors, iron bars, crystal beads and Indian cowries. [3]
   d) On the coast of Africa (the Gold Coast). [1]
   e) Any suitable answer – it is the quality of supporting argument that is important. One mark for each valid point made, up to a maximum of three, e.g. In a society without writing, oral tradition is a strong and powerful way to recount history – it may be very accurate. It may have become corrupted over the centuries. If most people in Benin accepted it as true then it is probably quite accurate. It tells us the history of Benin from the point of view of the people of Benin, not the Europeans. [3]
   f) Any suitable answer – it is the quality of supporting argument that is important. One mark for each valid point made, up to a maximum of three, e.g. If it is closely based on descriptions of sailors then it gives us an image of Benin based on European visitors and their views. Perhaps the sailors' views were only part of what life was like in Benin. If it is largely made up

by Dapper then it is much less useful. If, overall, it seemed to fit in with other accounts written by visitors it would be useful. [3]
   g) Any suitable answer – it is the quality of supporting argument that is important. One mark for each valid point made, up to a maximum of three, e.g. Yes – reference to big houses, visitors were obviously impressed, wealthy enough to trade with Europeans on their own terms; the Edo invited Europeans to come to trade, it wasn't imposed on them; No – we need lots of other information to complete the picture, such as size of the country; how wealthy ordinary people were; the sources only focus on trade, nothing else. [3]

Pages 184–185

Qing China

1. a) Britain/France and China [2]
   b) Britain and France [1]
   c) It obtained the territory of Hong Kong [1]; it increased its sales of opium to people in China [1]; trade became easier because the treaty ports were opened up to European countries [1]. [3]
   d) It lost territory [1]; the government lost power to European countries [1]; it had no say in the trade of opium [1]. [3]

2. It was very one-sided – all the power was with the Europeans. [1]

3. Any three of: In 1793 Emperor Qianlong said 'Our land is so wealthy and prosperous that we possess all things. Therefore there is no need to exchange the produce of foreign barbarians for our own.' In other words, they thought they had everything so became isolated and fell behind; it was a question of attitude and arrogance, rather than practicalities. China fell behind the West in technology – especially weapons. The Industrial Revolution and free trade had made Britain rich and powerful. Cheap opium from India was widely used in China. Chinese traders had to pay for this in silver, making Britain wealthy. China's government was weak – there were frequent rebellions against the government. [3]

4. Any suitable answer – it is the quality of supporting argument that is important. One mark for each valid point made, up to a maximum of three, e.g. Britain: selling opium; using force; demanding free trade; China: not wanting to trade; isolation; not modernising. [3]

5. People in the West wanted to buy Chinese porcelain – it was fashionable and expensive [1]. Chinese workers made items especially for the West such as tea services and sugar bowls – items that the Chinese didn't use [1]. China was strong – and rich [1]. Later, factories in the West like Delft and Royal Worcester made the porcelain themselves – it was just as good and cheaper [1]. Industry in the West grew and China's economy weakened [1]. Same story as China itself – very rich and powerful in the 17th and 18th centuries; falls behind the West in the 19th century [1]. [6].

Pages 186–187

Mughal India

1. a) Any suitable answer, supported by reasons. One mark for each valid point made up to a maximum of three, e.g. Possibly – if it was painted in the early 17th century, the artist might have met him/known him; it may be a copy of existing portraits; he is dressed in typical rich Mughal clothes. Possibly not – if it is from the late 17th century then the artist would have had to rely on other sources; some

portraits are painted to enhance the subject rather than to reflect exactly what they looked like. **[3]**

b) Answers will vary, e.g. impressive army, efficient government, strong economy, religious tolerance; a lot of the emphasis in the source is on culture and learning **[1]**.

c) Any suitable answer, supported by reasons. One mark for each valid point made up to a maximum of three, e.g. Source A because we can see what he looked like (if it is accurate); it was painted around the time of his rule; it shows his face and clothes so you can get a feel for the type of person he was. Source B because the historian should have used lots of research and consulted a range of sources before reaching a conclusion based on the evidence. It also ties in with what we know about India under Akbar. **[3]**

d) Either answer is correct – it is the quality of supporting argument that is important. One mark for each valid point made, up to a maximum of three, e.g. Yes – he expanded the country; encouraged religious tolerance; oversaw a strong economy; supported learning and culture. No – there were others who made Mughal India powerful; we need to know more about them before we can decide. **[3]**

2. It is very different **[1]**. The Tudor period was all about religious conflict **[1]** – Protestant Edward and Catholic Mary had people killed who refused to worship as they ordered **[1]**; Elizabeth wasn't as bad, but people were still fined for not attending Anglican services **[1]**. **[4]**

3. Any suitable answer, supported by reasons. One mark for each valid point made up to a maximum of three, e.g. Yes – it is a terrific achievement **[1]** which deserves to be preserved for future generations **[1]**; it reflects the power and glory of the Mughals **[1]**; eight million people visit every year so it needs help to preserve it **[1]**. **[3]**

Pages 188–189

The West Indies: Fighting Back Against Slavery

1. **1791** French Government gives 'full citizenship to people of colour' (if wealthy enough) (G); **1791** Toussaint leads the first rebellion against slave owners (C); **1792** The rebels control 33 per cent of the island (E); **1794** the French Government abolishes slavery (A); **1801** Toussaint's forces control the whole island (D); **1801** French troops invade Haiti and capture Toussaint and take him to France as a prisoner (I); **1803** Toussaint dies in a French prison (B); **1804** French troops defeated (J); **1804** Haiti declares itself an independent country (H); **1807** Britain ends the slave trade (F) **[10]**

2. Any two of: wanted an end to slavery; in protest at the horrendous living and working conditions; inspired by the French Revolution and the Declaration of the Rights of Man. **[2]**

3. Any two of: united behind the leadership of Toussaint; Toussaint was a great general; yellow fever killed thousands of French troops; success in battle. **[2]**

4. Any two of: Haiti became the first independent country in the Caribbean; the colony had defeated a major power (France); it led to other rebellions in the Caribbean; it sent shockwaves around other European colonial Governments. **[2]**

5. Any suitable answer, supported by reasons. One mark for each valid point made up to a maximum of two, e.g. Yes – he led the uprising; he ruled the free areas; he kept the people united; he was a great man. No – he died in a French prison in 1803; Dessalines led the army to victory in 1804. **[2]**

Pages 190–205

Mixed Test-Style Questions

Page 190

1. One mark for each valid observation (5 marks maximum). Your answer might include the following observations:
   - It tells us that John Lilburne believed every man and woman was equal.
   - It tells us that intellectual ideas played a part in the Civil Wars.
   - It explains why some people were opposed to Charles and his belief in Divine Right.
   - It is John Lilburne's personal opinion – it doesn't tell us how many people supported (or opposed) his views.
   - The Civil Wars started in 1642 and lasted till 1649 (or 1651); this speech dates from 1647 – it covers only a tiny part of the Civil Wars.

2. One mark for each valid observation (5 marks maximum). Your answer might include the following observations:
   - It tells us Akbar was a conqueror.
   - It tells us Shah Jahan was a good ruler.
   - It suggests Shah Jahan was better than Akbar.
   - It is the opinion of the author and no one else.
   - The author lived through much of Shah Jahan's rule, but only knew Akbar by repute.
   - It does not tell us what Akbar did other than conquer lands.
   - We need to know much more about both rulers to be able to reach a decision.

Page 192

1. One mark for each valid observation (5 marks maximum). Your answer might include the following observations:
   Definitely:
   - The ship sails to Vigo in Spain on 26 August.
   - Passengers will then travel on to London by train.
   - The fare is only £75.
   - The ship is luxurious.
   Probably:
   - People are migrating to England from Jamaica.
   - There are spaces still available on the boat.
   Still need to find out:
   - How many people bought tickets for the voyage.
   - How people raised the £75 to buy a ticket.
   - What happened to these people when they arrived in London.

2. One mark for each valid observation (5 marks maximum). Your answer might include the following observations:
   - It describes the events of Friday 18 November 1870.
   - It tells us that many male students opposed women training as doctors.
   - It helps to explain why there were so few women doctors – many decided not to apply to train as doctors because of male opposition.
   - It doesn't tell us about events at other universities.
   - It doesn't tell us if Sophia managed to complete her training and become a doctor.

Page 194

1. One mark for each valid observation (5 marks maximum). Your answer might include the following observations:
   - What living conditions were like in peacetime/at home in England for soldiers – did they have medical care, etc.?

- What he means by 'quiet' sectors.
- What the diet/healthcare of soldiers in the trenches was like.
- Was everybody at home the same?
- Were all soldiers treated the same?

2. One mark for each valid observation (5 marks maximum). Your answer might include the following observations:

Quite useful:
- John Ball (a preacher) was one of the leaders of the revolt.
- It tell us that some people thought society was unfair and wanted change.
- It tells us 'naughty men' were blamed for the ills of society.

Not very useful:
- It is only one part of the story.
- The sermon was delivered at Blackheath where the peasants had assembled to meet the king.
- It doesn't tell us what had happened before or after that.

Page 196

1. One mark for each valid observation (5 marks maximum). Your answer might include the following observations:
   - It was written by scientists.
   - It tells us what many scientists thought – and why.
   - It shows divisions among the scientists over whether or not to drop the bomb.
   - It explains the reasons for their thinking.
   - It comes down (marginally) in favour of using the atom bomb.
   - It shows the decision was not clear cut or easy to make.

2. One mark for each valid observation (5 marks maximum). Your answer might include the following observations:
   - It tells us that there was an official government response to the issue – a Board of Health made recommendations on how to recognise and treat cholera.
   - It tells us action was taken to reassure people, and to try to deal with the disease.
   - It describes the symptoms of cholera.
   - It gives a range of remedies.
   - The suggested remedies tell us that they didn't really know how to treat the disease.

Mark Scheme A

Marks are awarded as follows:

Simple, fragmentary answer: **1–2 marks.**

Fuller answer with more description: **3–4 marks.**

Full description with partial explanation: **5–6 marks.**

Full description and explanation, supported by some evidence: **7–8 marks.**

Full explanation and description, fully supported by evidence: **9–10 marks.**

Page 198

For marks for these questions see Mark Scheme A.

1. Your answer might include the following changes, backed up with explanation and facts:
   - from wood to stone
   - from defence to living places
   - taller, crenulated walls

- rounded corners to towers to make them stronger
- inner and outer bailey.

2. Your answer might include the following points, backed up with explanation and facts. Don't forget to emphasise the problems you face.
   - Seasonal activities – plough, sow, harvest, market, etc.
   - Difficulties might include warfare in the area; working unpaid for the lord of the manor several days a week; the need to make communal decisions in open field villages; disease and sickness – both human and animals; shortage of fertiliser; probably having to share a plough team; tithe for the Church.

3. Your answer should include the main events of the battle, backed up with explanation and facts:
   - Don't forget to explain why Parliament won – advantage of the high ground; Cromwell and his cavalry occupied the flanks; Prince Rupert's cavalry was defeated and ran; 4000 Royalists killed against 300 parliamentarians; discipline of the army.

Page 200

For marks for these questions see Mark Scheme A.

1. Your answer might include the following points, backed up with explanation and facts:

Yes:
- Many ships sailed from Europe to Africa, to the Americas and back to Europe.
- Some trade was from North America to Africa to the Caribbean and back to North America.
- The most profitable trade was the triangular trade, where profits were made on all legs, despite huge losses of slaves at sea.

No:
- Some trade was between Europe and Africa.
- Some trade was from North America to the Caribbean.

2. Your answer might include the following points, backed up with explanation and facts:
   - Once trains started to run, the country needed to all be on the same time, not sun-time as previously. This was known as railway time.
   - Faster journeys were possible.
   - Costs of travel and transport were reduced.
   - The railways helped to build up a national economy.
   - Daily national newspapers could be sent around the country more quickly, making the country more connected.
   - New suburban towns were developed within commuter distance to cities.

3. Your answer might include the following points, backed up with explanation and facts:
   - Long-term causes – such as alliances; the emergence of Germany as a major power; imperialism caused tensions between European powers; nationalism.
   - Short-term causes – military spending and Dreadnoughts; problems in the Balkans.
   - Trigger cause – assassination in Sarajevo.
   - War would probably have happened in due course without the assassination.

Page 202

For marks for these questions see Mark Scheme A.

1. Your answer might include the following reasons, backed up with explanation and facts. Don't forget to explain which reason you think was most important.
   - Careful planning – refusing to rush the invasion of Europe despite Stalin's demands.

- Air superiority.
- Deception – persuading Hitler the invasion would not be in Normandy.
- Technical ingenuity.
- Allied coordination.

2. Your answer might include the following, backed up with explanation and facts.
   - Provides 'cradle to the grave' help.
   - Ensures access to doctors, dentists and opticians.
   - Free hospital treatment.
   - Counters the 'Five Giants of Evil' identified in the Beveridge report.
   - Provides a financial 'safety net' of support for those who need it.
   - But very expensive – there is debate about whether the state can afford it.

3. Your answer might include the following, backed up with explanation and facts.
   - Youth culture completely changed – clothes and pop music.
   - Incredible atmosphere.
   - Made lots of money for UK in exports.
   - The contraceptive pill allowed changes to sexual behaviour.
   - BUT not for everyone or everywhere – things changed in London and many other places, but many people were 'passed by' by much of the sixties.

Page 204

For marks for these questions see Mark Scheme A.

1. Your answer might include the following points, backed up with explanation and facts.
   - 1530 – a strong empire, able to set its own terms with relatively weak European powers; Europe wanted Benin's goods; didn't allow Europeans free access to Benin.
   - 1730 – Western influence much stronger; other African countries getting richer through the slave trade and acquiring guns; Benin now relatively weaker; Benin no longer able to set the terms of trade.

2. Your answer might include the following points, backed up with explanation and facts.
   - 'Nanny of the Maroons' was a great leader.
   - The rough terrain/marginal lands where the Maroons lived was hard for the British to gain access into.
   - The Maroons were very determined to keep their hard-won freedom.
   - It was a difficult climate for European soldiers.
   - Maroons agreed to help British if Spain/France attacked Jamaica.
   - Maroons agreed not to help slaves escape or take in any further runaway slaves.

3. Your answer might include the following points, backed up with explanation and facts.
   - Sophia was a rich Indian princess, independent and determined. She gave lots of money to the cause.
   - She sold *The Suffragette* outside Hampton Royal Palace.
   - As goddaughter of Queen Victoria she attracted publicity.
   - She helped peacefully (the Suffragists) and violently (the Suffragettes) but was never sent to prison because of who she was.
   - Everyone wasn't one or the other – some supporters helped both organisations at times.
   - There is no 'typical' suffragette – rich and poor, famous and not famous all worked for the vote for women.

Acknowledgements

The authors and publisher are grateful to the copyright holders for permission to use quoted materials and images.

P5 © Illustrated London News Ltd/Mary Evans; P11 © UPPA/Photoshot; P21: The original uploader was Bunchofgrapes at English Wikipedia. (https://commons.wikimedia.org/wiki/File:Bubonic_plague_map_2.png#file), "Bubonic plague map 2", adapted key and labels, https://creativecommons.org/licenses/by-sa/3.0/legalcode; P30 © The Picture Art Collection / Alamy Stock Photo; P37 © Mary Evans Picture Library; P50 © Classic Image/Alamy; P58 © liszt collection/Alamy; P58 © Classic Image/Alamy; P59 © Mary Evans Picture Library/Alamy; P68 © The Art Gallery Collection/Alamy; P69 © Look and Learn; P90 © Image Asset Management Ltd/Alamy; P91 © Mary Evans Picture Library; P92 Extract from *Aspects of History – Britain 1750-1900: Industry, Trade & Politics* by Chris Andrews (Nelson Thornes, 2002) by S Pickering (OUP, 1965), reprinted by permission of the publishers, Oxford University Press; P102 © CPA Media Pte Ltd / Alamy Stock Photo; SBS Eclectic Images / Alamy Stock Photo; P103 © Peter Horree / Alamy Stock Photo; P104 © Guangsong Chen / Alamy Stock Photo; INTERFOTO / Alamy Stock Photo; P106 © GRANGER - Historical Picture Archive / Alamy Stock Photo; P107 © Steve Allen Travel Photography / Alamy Stock Photo; P108 © Chronicle / Alamy Stock Photo; Janusz Pieńkowski / Alamy Stock Photo; P109 © GL Archive / Alamy Stock Photo; P110 © Thomas Theodor Heine/DACS; P111 Extract from Winston Churchill's *Their Finest Hour* speech in June 1940; P116 © Neil Kenlock; P118 © Ancient Art & Architecture Collection Ltd/Alamy; P122 © Science Museum/Science & Society Picture Library; P151 © The Print Collector / Alamy Stock Photo; P161 © Nikreates / Alamy Stock Photo; Charles Stirling / Alamy Stock Photo; Nikreates /Alamy Stock Photo; P177 © reproduced by permission of Church Action on Poverty (www.church-poverty.org.uk); P179 © Copyright Guardian News & Media Ltd 2022; P181 © Powerhouse Museum collection. Designer and photographer unknown; P186 © Signal Photos / Alamy Stock Photo; P188 © Hi-Story / Alamy Stock Photo; P192 ©TfL from the London Transport Museum collection; P196 © Broadsheet warning about Indian cholera 1831. Wellcome Collection. All other images © Shutterstock.com

Every effort has been made to trace copyright holders and obtain their permission for the use of copyright material. The authors and publisher will gladly receive information enabling them to rectify any error or omission in subsequent editions. All facts are correct at time of going to press.

Published by Collins
An imprint of HarperCollins*Publishers*
1 London Bridge Street
London SE1 9GF

HarperCollins*Publishers*
Macken House
39/40 Mayor Street Upper
Dublin 1
D01 C9W8
Ireland

© HarperCollins*Publishers* Limited 2023

ISBN 9780008551490

First published 2023

10 9 8 7 6 5 4 3

British Library Cataloguing in Publication Data.

A CIP record of this book is available from the British Library.

Publishers: Katie Sergeant and Clare Souza
Commissioning: Richard Toms
Authors: Philippa Birch, Steve McDonald, Rachelle Pennock and Alf Wilkinson
Project managed by Cambridge Publishing Management Ltd, Shelley Teasdale and Fiona Watson
Cover Design: Kevin Robbins and Sarah Duxbury
Inside Concept Design: Sarah Duxbury and Paul Oates
Text Design and Layout: Jouve India Private Limited
Production: Emma Wood
Printed in India by Multivista Global Pvt. Ltd.